Tim Dale

Harrods

The Store and the Legend

Pan Original
Pan Books London and Sydney

Permissions
The author and publishers wish to thank the *New Standard* for permission
to use the two cartoons which appear on pages 134 and 139.

First published 1981 by Pan Books Ltd,
Cavaye Place, London SW10 9PG
© Tim Dale 1981
ISBN 0 330 26344 7
Printed in Great Britain by
Richard Clay (The Chaucer Press) Ltd, Bungay, Suffolk

for my wife, Pat

Contents

List of illustrations

Acknowledgements

So many people have provided help and information to me in writing this book that it is tempting to thank everyone in the store and leave it at that. However, that would be an in·ustice as there are some who have gone out of their way to help and given freely of their knowledge and experience.

First and foremost I must thank Mr Aleck Craddock. It was his approval and support that enabled me to get the project off the ground in the first place and without his continued interest and guidance it would still be just a good idea on the drawing board. I am very much in his debt.

The other people I would like to thank specifically are:
George Boobyer, the buyer of the photographic department
Cliff Bulcock, chief engineer
Phillip Burrows, manager of the safe deposit
Ted Coleman, assistant to the director of merchandise
Douglas Cross, power plant manager
Walter Cooper, service manager
Debbie Cozens, my former secretary
Richard Furnival Jones, department sales manager in wines
  and spirits
Tony Guyatt, section manager of the food halls
John McKitterick, the display manager
Mrs W. Miln, wife of the former food section manager
Murray Miln, the son of Mrs W. Miln and himself food
  section manager
Sandy Murray, buyer of the suit room on the fashion floor
Compton Nascimento, the despatch manager
Pat Newell, first floor divisional manager
Frank Nichols, the chief security officer

Leonard Pitkin, former assistant to the personnel manager
Cliff Shinn, the chief cashier
Rita Stratta, the pet shop buyer
Roger Street, the glass buyer
Heather Summerfield, the press relations officer
Alistair Walker, divisional manager of the food halls

Two people I would particularly like to thank for their enthusiastic and invaluable help are:
Bert White, the assistant controller of store services who has worked in the store since 1937 and, in recent years, made a detailed survey of the development of the store building; the plans showing the development of the store from 1849 to 1911 are his work. He also kindly showed me a project on the history of Harrods written by his daughter, Zoe.

Jim Beedham, the assistant chief engineer who keeps in his office a fascinating collection of Harrods memorabilia to which he allowed me free access. He is also the person who provided most of the more obscure statistics.

Last but certainly not least, John Talbot of Pan Books and Geoffrey Van Dantzig, the Harrods book buyer, who together with my wife Pat hatched the idea of this book in the first place.

CHAPTER ONE

Enter a different world

'Right, Johnnie, what is the capital of France?'
'Paris.'
'What is the capital of Italy?'
'Rome.'
'What is the capital of England?'
'Harrods.'
Small boy in geography class

There are larger stores in the world; not many, just one or two. There are more modern stores; there are some with a longer history but, when all is said and done, it is unique, the most famous of all, the Rolls-Royce of stores, in a class by itself. It is Harrods.

Harrods is about merchandise. The latest and most exciting, the traditional and proven; items just that little bit different are displayed in such a way and in such quantity as to leave the spectator overwhelmed. From the 450 cheeses to the 350 suites of furniture, from the 150 pianos to the 8,000 dresses, Harrods offers the customer a diversity and volume of choice that takes the breath away.

Harrods is about selling on a grand scale. Ask a normal retailer how much selling space he has and he will answer you in square feet; ask Harrods and they will answer you in acres, fourteen acres with a choice of 220 selling departments, as well as further acres of warehouses, workshops, stockrooms and offices. Harrods is like an iceberg; what can be seen is less than half the story. There is a five-storey building at Trevor Square across the Brompton Road, and at Barnes, furniture depositories, an auction gallery and the Harrodian Club.

Harrods is about service. Customers may pay on the spot in cash at one of the 500 cash registers or they may choose to join that select club of 150,000 people who have an account with the store. They may take their purchase with them, they may have it delivered by one of the sixty green vans or it can be sent by rail, sea or air to anywhere in the world. They may bank with Harrods, insure with Harrods, buy, rent or sell their home through Harrods, borrow books from the largest commercial private library in the country; they may arrange their holiday through Harrods, eat in one of Harrods' seven restaurants and, when the time comes, the funerals department will take care of the final journey.

Harrods is about people. Customers in millions each year spending hundreds of millions of pounds in tens of millions of transactions. A payroll of 5,000 rising to 6,000 at Christmas time and sale periods costs millions in wages alone.

Harrods is about exporting. Over one hundred years ago the slogan of the store was 'Harrods Serves The World' and that was never more true than it is today. No other store has such an international reputation and millions of pounds worth of trade each year is conducted on an export basis. Harrods bags have been sighted aboard the QE2 and on Concorde, on Hong Kong junks and Mississippi steamers, on safari in the Serengeti and on climbing expeditions up Mount Everest. Jimmy Carter returning from a visit to Great Britain disembarked from Air Force One at Washington airport carrying a Harrods bag. Alternatively, they can be found lining the waste bins of houses in the Greater London area.

The range of merchandise exported makes interesting reading: a Persian rug to Persia; French wine to France; a refrigerator to Finland; a gazebo to Saudi Arabia; a handkerchief to Los Angeles – the handkerchief cost thirty-five pence and the air freight £17.50; a replica of a 1901 Ford to an Arab sheik; a fossil excavated in Texas, bought by Harrods and sold to a Texan for re-export to Texas.

Harrods is about self-sufficiency; it still manufactures

some of the merchandise it sells and it generates most of the
18 million units of electricity it uses each year. It draws
water from its own wells, 250 feet below the store.

'Enter a different world' is the current Harrods slogan;
the question is how? There are eleven entrances for customers which can cause problems when you've said to a
friend that you'll meet at the 'main entrance'.

The problem could really start earlier than this with
parking the car. You can make for one of two car parks.
The first is Harrods' own in a little cul-de-sac called Brompton Place which is a turning off the southern side of Brompton Road. If this is full there is another car park owned by
NCP just off Basil Street. It is linked to Harrods by a tunnel
and you emerge via a spiral staircase into the Man's Shop.

Of the eleven entrances two are recommended to Harrods beginners – Door 5 and Door 10. Door 10 is at the
west end of the store and leads into the pharmacy department. Door 5 leads into the escalator hall. The escalators
are by far the best way of getting from floor to floor since
the lifts never seem to be on the floor that you are. Secondly,
there are plenty of signs and directions informing you
where you want to be.

Of the eleven entrances two are recommended to Harrods is to realize that the trunk routes all run east to west
and vice versa. Only a native with generations of instinct
stands any chance of a successful north to south crossing.
For all others it is sheer folly, many have disappeared without trace in the complex maze of the stationery department,
expired in despair behind a jewellery cabinet, or perished
wandering in the desolate wastes of the Central Hall. All of
them could have been saved if they had only known to stick
to the east–west passage. Doors 5 and 10 set you up for a
successful safari.

There is always a Green man on Door 5, officially known
as a Harrods commissionaire, and he can be a real blessing
if you have an armful of parcels and are the sort of person
whom taxi drivers customarily ignore. Green men are
chosen from applicants at least six feet three inches tall who

possess endless charm and tact, can conjure a taxi out of thin air, can melt a female traffic warden with a devastating smile and paralyse with fear her male counterpart. It's the sort of job Rock Hudson or Gregory Peck might get on a day when there was not the usual competition. Also Esther Rantzen interviews passers-by outside Door 5 for her television programme 'That's Life'. As a way of letting your friends know that you shop at Harrods it definitely has more class than carrying a Harrods carrier bag at the local supermarket.

Each floor tends to be devoted to certain categories of merchandise. You may of course rely on the staff for directions but perhaps it is as well to remember that 5,000 new staff start at Harrods each year and most of them spend the greater part of their first few weeks trying to find their own department, let alone taking on your problems as well. The chances of picking on one of these when you ask for help is statistically not high but in practice you never miss. The experienced staff can smell a lost customer several yards away and keep right out of range; this is not because they are inherently unhelpful but rather it is a natural reaction to years of being asked for directions, patiently providing the answer and then watching the customer walk off in the opposite direction.

By far the best course of action is to accept that you are on your own and to become a Harrods expert; the satisfaction of being able to walk around the store free from the nagging doubts about where you are and where you are going is its own reward.

CHAPTER TWO

The history of Harrods

Harrods was not always the colossus it is today; like all mighty oaks it grew from a very small acorn indeed.

Henry Charles Harrod was born in 1800 and started his working life as a miller in Clacton. He married Elizabeth Digby, the daughter of a pork butcher. The couple moved to Cable Street, Stepney in 1835 where Harrod started a business as a wholesale grocer and tea dealer. The business prospered and in 1849 he opened new premises at 38 Eastcheap. Amongst his customers was a certain Philip Henry Burden. Besides doing business together the two men appear to have become friends as there seems to be no other explanation for Harrod's subsequent behaviour. Burden's shop was at No. 8 Middle Queen's Buildings which was situated in the Brompton Road in a somewhat unsalubrious district between Hyde Park Corner and Kensington known as Knightsbridge.

Knightsbridge itself is named after a bridge which crossed the River Westbourne at a point where Albert Gate and the French Embassy stand today. There seems to have been some sort of settlement near the place since the thirteenth century but perhaps the building of barracks in Hyde Park in the first half of the nineteenth century led to a very modest shopping development in Brompton Road; along with Mr Burden's small grocery shop there were two cobblers, an apothecary and a draper as well as some professional men.

Philip Burden had been in financial difficulty for some time and Harrod began to help him by paying the rent and not pressing for payments. The exact moment when Mr Burden gave up the unequal struggle to stay in business is a little difficult to establish. 1849 has for many years been accepted as the year of the founding of Harrods but from the available records it is apparent that Harrod did not become the owner of Burden's shop premises until 1853. A possible explanation is that Harrod's interest in Burden's shop gradually increased over a period of years as he provided greater financial help. The great cholera epidemic of 1848/9 may have been an influential factor in persuading Harrod to move away from the City of London to a small 'country' shop in Knightsbridge.

Shortly after taking over Burden's business, Harrod moved from Eastcheap to live 'over the shop'. The most famous name in retailing was born. To this day Harrods has not forgotten that it started life as a grocer and the grocery department now called the Pantry is department number one, or department 0001 as it has now become in deference to the computer's predilection for four digit numbers. Harrods is, in fact, the only major department store to have started as a grocer; many of the others began as drapers.

The Great Exhibition of 1851, held in Hyde Park, had the effect of turning Knightsbridge into a much more fashionable residential area and development westwards along the Cromwell Road took place, together with the building of South Kensington's fine Gothic Victorian museums. However, it seems that Henry Harrod was more intent on a quiet life and a steady business than founding a legend. The shop changed little in its early years and was largely dependent on an 'over-the-counter' trade in tea which was natural in light of Harrod's previous career.

Charles Digby Harrod, his son, was a man of greater energy and had the vision to see the potential of the shop and to begin driving forward to greater things. He was born in 1841 and at the age of sixteen was sent to the City to work in a grocer's shop, where he learnt the trade. The first lesson that he received in business came from his father and was to the effect that nothing of value comes for free. The shop was not given by father to son; it was sold to him in 1861 in a transaction that stipulated payment over a period of years. Whether this made a strong impression on the young Harrod, who was then in his twenties, is not known but what is certain is that he denied his customers credit for the next twenty years.

They were prosperous years for England and gradually the shop began to flourish. Harrods would not have achieved its position of pre-eminence without the efforts of some remarkable men and Charles Digby Harrod was certainly the first in this distinguished line. His nature was to lead from the front and he never asked his employees to take on any task that he himself was not prepared to do. His customers found him 'so handsome, so honest and so obliging' that he soon built up a fine reputation for himself in the neighbourhood. He had a brother, who also worked in the business until 1866, before deciding to move on.

Victorian Knightsbridge was a very different place from the Knightsbridge we know today. It was the age of the cobbled street and the horse drawn carriage, of typhoid fever and cholera and of muck, soot and fog in London's streets. At this period Charles Dickens was writing in *Bleak House* of 'smoke lowering down from chimney pots, making soft black drizzle, with flakes of soot in it as big as full grown snow flakes ... Dogs indistinguishable in mire. Horses scarcely better; splashed to their very blinkers. Foot passengers jostling one another's umbrellas, in a general infection of ill-temper, and losing their foothold at street corners, where tens of thousands of other foot passengers have been slipping and sliding since the day broke ...' Small wonder then that the proliferation of murky alleys that riddled the area around Mr Harrod's shop were rife with petty criminals, to whom thieving was the only recourse from their abject poverty with no social security to keep them above the threshold of survival.

There is no doubt Charles Digby was an extremely hard-working and ambitious man. His working day began well before 8.00 a.m. He expected similar dedication from his staff whom he stipulated should arrive for work with clean faces; but he was not without a human side and on several occasions, when seeing one of his regular customers in some financial embarrassment, was known to instruct his salesman, 'See that she has what she needs and send the bill to me.'

His fiercest commercial battle was fought with the Co-operatives – a very potent force at this time. They represented a real threat to the small independent retailer because of their ability to offer discount prices. The small man's recourse was usually to depend upon cook's bribes; these were payments to the servants of the gentry to encourage them to put the trade of their masters the way of the payer's shop. Another device was that of allowing easy and extended credit, which permitted the servant, whose master was not in the know, to have use of the money in the meantime.

However, Charles Digby Harrod would have none of this nonsense, which he adjudged immoral, and stipulated cash on the nail. Further, he declined to employ barkers to attract custom, preferring to circulate lists of the produce on offer to the finer houses in the area.

His approach paid off as, without having to finance other people's credit, he was able to compete keenly on price. By 1864 he had cleared his debt to his father, who shortly afterwards retired to 9 Thurloe Place in Knightsbridge, close by. Meanwhile the address of the shop had changed from 8 Middle Queen's Buildings to No. 105 Brompton Road. In 1864 also, at the age of twenty-three, Charles Digby Harrod married the daughter of a fellow grocer.

Four years later turnover had reached £1,000 a week and more space was urgently needed. Harrod decided to move, first to Esher and then to Sydenham and the space thus gained was turned to good use in the business. A new shop front which was fitted allowed perfumery, medicine and stationery departments to be added. A two-storey extension in what had been his garden was built to give additional space used to sell flowers, fruit and vegetables and cooked meats.

The enlarged business required additional management and Charles Digby was joined by his cousin William Kibble. Kibble had been widowed and while he was recovering had moved out to Clapham to stay with a Mr and Mrs Viney, owners of Clapham Stores. Kibble learned the food business there and quickly proved himself a great asset to Harrod; the fruit and vegetables which he brought back each day from the market at Covent Garden soon gained a reputation as the best in the neighbourhood. His connection with Harrods saw the beginning of an association between the Knightsbridge shop and Clapham Stores which was to last into the present century.

In 1874 the adjoining premises was acquired and a new facade went up bearing the lettering 'HARROD'S STORES' for the first time. In the same year Charles Digby started a van delivery service, the running costs of which added considerably to the outgoings, which included a weekly payroll of £15. 101 and 103 Brompton Road were taken over and converted to shop premises.

Harrod employed 100 people by 1880 and three years later over 150. The store was further expanded, and was then also selling china, glass, ironmongery and turnery. Turnery is merchandise carved on a turning lathe such as table lamps and there was a department of that name in Harrods until the late 1960s.

Christmas 1883 promised to be the best yet and by early December the store was overflowing with merchandise in readiness for the rush. Many stores, especially those in America, were experimenting with electrically-lit window displays but Harrod was traditional in some of his ways, and in his store gas jets burned all night, partly to illuminate the merchandise and partly to put off the local burglars.

It was a foul winter's night on 6 December with temperatures below freezing and snow borne on a howling wind. William Kibble was last out of the shop, together with a faithful servant of the company, Mr Gearing. Whether the curtains blew into the gaslight jet on account of the high wind or whether workmen in the basement had left a candle burning which caught alight is debatable, but what is certain is that Mr Gearing was awoken at midnight to be told that Harrod's Stores was burning. His account in the archives of the company tells how he at once went round, and on seeing how serious the fire was, despatched Gamble, another assistant, in a hansom to fetch Harrod from Sydenham. Gearing watched the fire all night; Harrod arrived about six in the morning.

The *Chelsea Herald* of Saturday, 8 December reported the incident at considerable length and with a flamboyance bordering on relish which brings the scene vividly to life:

'Harrod's stores are now a heap of ruins, and with those buildings other establishments which adjoined – those of Mr Jeffcoat, brushmaker, and Mr de Costa, draper, have been much injured ... The alarm was raised shortly before midnight and at half past one in the morning the fire was at its height. From the raised pavement on the west side of Brompton Road a considerable crowd watched a scene of a splendidly terrible character. Only the skeleton of the three large shops and the stores at the back remained, but the fire raged in a seething mass, shooting high up in the air from the inner portion, whilst the flames clung tenaciously to the window frames, mouldings and other woodwork, thus outlining the structure as if by an intentional illumination. The steam fire engine and hose from the hydrants were pouring tons of water upon the burning mass with no apparent effect in even checking the conflagration.

'Meantime in the rear, the scene was of a most exciting character. The wind blew the sparks in clouds, and at length the flames, right over the cottages in Queen's Gardens, and across North Street and even as far as Hans Place. The occupants of the cottages in Queen's Gardens were so terrified that some of them moved their goods into the street, whilst women and children were running about excitedly and crying in their terror. Shortly before two a.m. there was a terrific rush of flame from the rear of the stores, caused apparently by the ignition of a quantity of spirits or other inflammables. The fearful heat thrown out by this caused a general stampede of all who were near the fire, which at that moment seemed to threaten with destruction the whole range of private dwellings. Fortunately, however, this was averted. Enormous quantities of water were poured upon the part which connected the business premises with the cottages and thus the latter were saved. The water, moreover, soon had a perceptible effect on the principal seat of the fire, for by half past two the fire brigade had obtained complete mastery over it. Between three and four o'clock it was difficult to approach the ruins owing to the smoke and steam that rose up in clouds from the smouldering mass.

'The effect produced in the sky by the fire was most remarkable. Heavy clouds now hung over western London, and the reflection of the flames upon them, as seen from the Strand, resembled in its brilliant grandeur some of those phenomenal sunsets which have lately excited general attention.'

Harrod's customers shortly received a letter from him.

> Harrod's Stores,
> 101/103/105 Brompton Road
> 7 December 1883

Madam,
I greatly regret to inform you that, in consequence of the above premises being burnt down, your order will be delayed in the execution a day or two. I hope, in the course of Tuesday or Wednesday next, to be able to forward it.

In the meantime may I ask you for your kind indulgence.
Your obedient servant,
C. D. Harrod.
PS All communications to be addressed to 78, Brompton Road.

It is said that Charles Digby Harrod refused to be defeated by the disaster and found temporary premises opposite his ruined store from which he penned the letter and proceeded to fill his Christmas orders. In spite of the fire, 1883 was the best year to date for Christmas trade. The enclosure from the *Draper* sent in a letter written to William Kibble forty-eight years after the event by a contemporary employee named Mr Wallis Fraser, of Fulham in London, tells a different story:

The Stranger in the Bus

One day, Edgar Cohen, then in the sponge business, was going home in an omnibus when a stranger asked him to lend him half a sovereign, saying he had lost his purse and giving him his card, which bore the name of Charles Harrod, and when Cohen obliged, asked for one of his.

When the money was returned the next day Cohen forgot the incident until many months later, a woman's voice spoke to him on the telephone saying she was Mrs Harrod and imploring him to come over and see her husband, who was heartbroken because his store had been burned down.

Store in a Market

Harrod, who was almost prostrate with grief, asked Cohen to take charge. Cohen went to the Haymarket Stores and asked them to deal with all Harrod's orders, putting Harrod's labels on the parcels, and otherwise doing the business as though it was their own.

Then going to the site of a Japanese market which had just closed down near Harrod's in Brompton Road, he rented it and opened there a temporary Harrod's until the real store was rebuilt.

At the time of this article, 1931, the Haymarket Stores were taken over by Harrods, ironically.

Rebuilding on the same site began at once and the new premises were opened in September 1884. Perhaps Harrod was touched by the loyalty of his customers during this period, for shortly afterwards he allowed the first credit accounts to be opened, Amongst the original few selected for this honour were Lily Langtry, Oscar Wilde and Ellen Terrey. The rebuilt store is described by 'The Baron' in The *Chelsea Herald* of 30 August 1884.

As we enter from the street we are struck by the vast area that opens to our view, but we proceed at once to the basement and here we find strong rooms where the silver goods kept in stock can be placed safely after closing hours; here too are cellars built purposely for the storing of sugar, others for provisions, and bins by the score for the varied assortment of wines and spirits. There are also tea rooms piled up with chests from the lowly 'mixed at two shillings per pound' to the aristocratic 'scented pekoe' and another 'all the sweet perfumes of Arabia' containing the spices and other condiments of an appetizing nature.

Ascending, we are in the 'shop', and in the centre we see a large circular counter where orders are to be written out and instructions given to a staff of clerks specially appointed for the purpose. On the left there are the wines, and we find a stock assorted to suit the tastes of all opponents of total abstinence. There are clarets from 'ordinaire' to high class Chateau productions, ports of the vintages sacred to those who have no dread of the gout, and selected from the best shipments of Cockburn, Kopke, Graham, Morgan and others. Champagnes from that bearing the very broad description 'superior' up to such luxurious drinks as Giesler, Mumm, Perinet, Piper or Pommery, while for those of smaller means or semi-abstainers there are the exhilarating but somewhat saccharine liquors that owe their origin to fruits grown on British soil. Then there are spirits called not 'from the vasty deep' – for water is a matter that when Gin, Brandy, Rum or Whisky are concerned Mr Harrod prefers to leave to the discretion of his customers – but there are those of the mineral class from soda to the medicinal Carlsbad, Schlossbunnen, Taunas and some which are surely bottled for the fair sex namely, Mesdames and Celestines.

Stretching from here for a long way into the distance is the tea and grocery counter where pyramids of tea and sugar, mountains of coffee are mixed up with tins of biscuits, breeches' paste, blancmange, glycerine, lobsters, plate powder, sugar candy, boot top powder, wax vestas, salt, prawns, phosphor paste, oysters, milk, knife polish, house flannel, dog biscuits, mustard and a thousand and one other articles of a heterogeneous nature, but all of which meet in the store room of any well ordered household.

Next on the right comes the fruit and flower department and here is to be a collection that will hold its own against any of the Covent Garden shops, while in flowers there are to be daily supplies of shrubs and blooming plants, nor are the beaux' and belles' requirements in the shape of bouquets and 'buttonholes' to be forgotten.

Beyond this is the 'stall' where poultry and game are to be

on view, and we are informed that arrangements have been made for a constant and daily supply direct from the country so that the handling, packing and repacking which is so objectionable but which it is impossible to prevent with ordinary market-bought produce will be entirely avoided, and to complete this side of the place there is a long counter where cheeses from America, the foreign Gruyère, Chapzugar Camembert and the delicious productions of Wilts are to be found. Here too will be seen the goods comprised under the heading 'general provisions', such as Australian meats, bacon, butter – not bosch – and hams from York, Ireland, Canada, or Westphalia.

As we look around this ground floor we are quite surprised at the enormous quantities of each article that it appears necessary to keep ready, but it is explained that often, and more particularly at holiday times and on Saturdays, there is such a rush of customers that unless this precaution was taken it would be impossible to serve quickly enough to keep the place even moderately clear.

In the middle of this floor is a grand staircase wide enough for five or six persons to ascend or descend abreast and this takes us to a spacious warehouse where we find an amazing show of sterling silver and electro goods, and being all perfectly new and freshly unpacked the effect is somewhat more than one would expect to find in any retail establishment of ordinary dimensions.

There are spoons and forks of all sorts, tea services, trays, biscuit boxes, soup tureens, kettles and stands, but a very noticeable feature is a splendid assortment of the goods that are now somewhat the rage, namely, jugs, flagons, salad bowls, trays, etc. made of oak and mounted in electro. These of themselves are worth seeing, and will, we doubt not, attract a good many people to take a lounge on this floor.

But this is not all that is to be found here, for there is a big show of lamps, from those burning benzoline and costing a few pence, to the delicately painted china varieties, for the drawing room or boudoir, and as a direct contrast there are lanterns for stable use and the burglar's bull's-eye.

Around the wall are cases for saddlery, and the stock comprises everything from the donkey's pad to the racing saddle, or from the halter to a set of four-horse harness, while further on there are boxes, portmanteaux, overland trunks, hat cases, in fact travelling luxuries of every conceivable shape and size. To the left there are the modern brass goods comprising high class fenders, fire irons, coal boxes, and beyond are kitchen requisites and turnery, mats, brushes, etc. The whole of this spacious floor is under the management of Mr Smart, and he is to be congratulated on having produced a show that, being almost unique in this class of business, deserves to be fully patronized by all who visit his employer's new premises.

One flight higher and we are in a portion of the building that is sure to find favour with the gentler sex, for here are displayed all sorts of fancy requisites for the toilet, perfumes from the laboratories of Atkinson, Piesse, and Rimmel, together with the countless odds and ends in the way of cosmetiques that are eagerly sought after by those who indulge in 'paint, powder, and patches'. Then comes a stock of articles equally or even more necessary, but not quite so much sought after, namely, patent medicines, and arrangements have been perfected with a competent dispenser in the neighbourhood so that prescriptions at store prices can be made up without delay.

After all this realism, turning to something of a lighter character we find ourselves surrounded by games of all sorts – croquet, billiards, chess boards and the racing game, and another bearing the somewhat wild title of 'Go-bang'. There are also coupelette, magic skittles, tareteer, la poule, knock-em-downs, and last, the dear old soul for whom we have such affection at holiday times, 'Old Aunt Sally'.

On the third floor we find iron and brass bedsteads and bedding suited for high, low, rich or poor, but on the way down we pass through a pair of iron doors to find ourselves in an immense place set apart for the exhibition of furniture, and thence into a huge reserve store of all the goods that are in daily requisition in the different departments.

Descending once more we are shown over the stables, where there are stalls and loose boxes for a large number of horses, together with standing room for carts, vans and hand trucks in endless variety; and with this our tour of inspection ends.

This report does show very clearly that by the time the store was rebuilt Charles Digby Harrod had developed out of all recognition the rather modest shop his father had sold to him just over twenty years before. It was now a store, and a sizeable one with a well-to-do clientele and 200 staff on its payroll.

However, it seems that the building of the new store had taken a lot out of Charles Digby Harrod; it was certainly a fitting finale to his career as a retailer, and as the 1880s wore on his thoughts turned towards retirement.

Henry Charles Harrod, the firm's founder, died at the age of eighty-five in 1885 and perhaps this event also contributed towards the decision to sell the store. So it was that in November 1889 Harrods was floated as a limited liability company and a copy of the original prospectus survives. The same Edgar Cohen, whom Charles Digby Harrod had met on a bus around the time the store burnt down, advised him in the conduct of the sale. Cohen bought the business and floated it, telling Harrod to take his money in £1 founder shares. Harrod replied, 'If I sell I retire. If I own shares I shall worry about the business, which will not be retirement.' The time did come subsequently when he did buy founder shares at £4 each, but by then the original shares had been split into hundredths, which meant that he bought for £400 a time what he had refused for £1. Although Cohen's name does not appear on the prospectus as a director, he nevertheless became one a few years later and retained the appointment until after 1912.

Under the management of the Mr Smart referred to in the prospectus, business and resulting profits seem to have been reduced considerably. This eventually culminated in the directors asking C. D. Harrod to return, which he did for a further eighteen months.

During this time he entrusted his friend Cohen with one last task – that of finding a general manager. Cohen eventually recommended a Richard Burbidge whom he knew had recently left William Whiteley's. Whiteley's was the largest department store in London and had been so for many years. Burbidge reputedly fell out with Whiteley because the latter is alleged to have held that no employee

The List of Applications opens on Tuesday, 26th November, and will be closed the same day at or before 4 p.m. for Town, and the following morning for the Country.

HARROD'S STORES, LIMITED.

Incorporated under the Companies Acts, 1862 to 1886, whereby the liability of the Shareholders is limited to the amount of their Shares.

CAPITAL—£141,400,

DIVIDED INTO

140,000 Ordinary Shares and 1,400 Founders' Shares of £1 each.

After payment in each year of a dividend at the rate of 8 per cent. on the Ordinary Shares, the surplus profits, subject to the provision of a reserve fund, will be divisible in equal moieties between the holders of the Ordinary and Founders' Shares.

The whole of the Founders' Shares and £75,000 of the Ordinary Shares have already been subscribed at par, in accordance with the terms of this prospectus, and will be allotted in full. and subscriptions are now invited at par for the balance of the Ordinary Shares payable as follows:—

5s. on Application.

15s. on Allotment.

Directors.

A. J. NEWTON, Esq. *(Chairman)*, 8, Leadenhall Street, E.C. (Chairman, Empire Palace, Limited).
JAMES BAILEY, Esq. (Proprietor of Bailey's Hotel and South Kensington Hotel).
H. BENNETT, Esq. (MARLER & BENNETT, Estate Agents), Sloane Street, S.W.
F. H. HARVEY-SAMUEL, Esq., 1, Whittington Avenue, E.C.
WILLIAM JOSEPH LAMB, Esq., 7, Philpot Lane, E.C.

Bankers.

THE LONDON AND COUNTY BANKING COMPANY, LIMITED, 31, Lombard Street, E.C., and Branches.

Solicitors.

Messrs. ASHURST, MORRIS, CRISP & CO., 6, Old Jewry, E.C.

Brokers.

Messrs. ELLIS & CO., 2, Royal Exchange Buildings, E.C.

Auditors.

Messrs. DELOITTE, DEVER, GRIFFITHS & CO., 4, Lothbury, E.C.

Secretary *(pro tem.)*

Mr. CLELAND HEYWOOD.

Temporary Offices.

47, Old Broad Street, E.C.

PROSPECTUS.

THIS COMPANY is formed to take over, carry on, and extend the well-known Harrod's Stores, in the Brompton Road.

The business, which was originally established by the father of Mr. C. D. Harrod, the present Vendor, has steadily and of late years rapidly developed ; the sales for the year ended Good Friday, 1889, amounted to £492,548, and except for the state of Mr. Harrod's health, which makes this step imperative, the opportunity of acquiring this business would not have presented itself.

The Company acquires the valuable and extensive leasehold premises in the Brompton Road, which are chiefly held for an unexpired term of 47 years, at the aggregate moderate rent of £1,635 a year; also the extensive warehouses on the east side of Queen's Gardens, Richmond Gardens and New Court, embracing a large area. These premises, a portion of which are sublet at about £400 per annum, are not only sufficiently commodious to carry on the present business, but afford ample accommodation for a large increase in the volume of trade which may confidently be looked for.

The Stores are admirably situated, having an extensive frontage to a most important thoroughfare, and adjacent to perhaps the largest residential neighbourhood of London.

The great advantage which as compared with other similar undertakings this Company will enjoy is that the Stores are free to the public, and unfettered by any restrictions as to tickets or otherwise.

The shares of the leading Co-operative Stores and Societies can only be held and dealt in by a limited class. The shares of this Company will have the great advantage of being marketable among the general public, although it is anticipated that they will be largely held by persons contributing to the trade of the Company, with a view to obtain the full benefit of the co-operative system by participating in the profits.

That a business of this kind readily lends itself to being conducted on co-operative principles is at once proved by the striking success of other similar companies, such as the Civil Service Stores Supply Association, the Army and Navy Stores, and others, the shares of which command large premiums and yield large and increasing dividends to the Shareholders.

Mr. Harrod's business is mainly in provisions and articles of daily household use, and not, therefore, liable to the fluctuations attending a business which is subject to the influences of fashion.

The books of the Vendor have been examined by Messrs. Deloitte, Dever, Griffiths & Co., the well-known Accountants; and in their report they say that the net profits of the business for the three years ended Good Friday, 1889, showed an average of nearly £16,000 per annum, and that the net profits for the last year, after allowing for depreciation, were £17,244, while to pay 8 per cent. on the Ordinary Shares will require only £11,200.

The turnover for the current year has again increased by over £400 a week, and, with the evidence of increasing trade before them, the Directors consider that an annual net profit of £20,000 may soon be anticipated. Such a result would not only suffice to pay the 8 per cent. dividend on the Ordinary Shares, but subject to the provision for the establishment of a Reserve Fund, would leave available a surplus of £8,800, or sufficient out of the proportion. attributable to the holders of the Ordinary Shares to pay them a further dividend of nearly 3 per cent., while, in the course of a few years, there is every reason to suppose that the turnover and profits of the Company will reach figures sufficient to pay even larger dividends.

The price to be paid by the Company for the entire properties, including plant, machinery, horses, vans, harness, fixtures, fittings, furniture of every description, the extensive leasehold premises above mentioned, and the goodwill, is £100,000, while the stock is to be taken over at cost.

The Vendor has consented to divide with the Company the profits made since the last stock-taking, and the Company's share has been fixed at the agreed sum of £5,000, which will be more than required to cover all expenses of the formation of the Company.

The capital of the Company will be sufficient to pay the purchase price, and provide, considering the nature of the business, ample working capital.

The business is acquired from the 2nd December, and from that date until taken over it will be carried on by the Vendor for the benefit and on account of the Company.

Arrangements have been made with the Vendor's present Manager, Mr. Smart, by which his services as Manager have been secured to the Company for a period of seven years.

The Founders' Shares have all been applied for, and will be allotted in full to the applicants, who, in consideration thereof, have provisionally subscribed the whole of the Ordinary Shares now issued, but except to the amount of the above mentioned £75,000 Ordinary Shares, no preference in the allotment will be given to these applications.

The Company will thus be enabled to commence its business with the subscription of the whole of the share capital assured.

No promotion money has been or will be paid. The purchase is made direct from Mr. Harrod, and the Company will have the very unusual advantage of commencing business without having its undertaking weighted with the profits of an intermediate Vendor.

A large number of Contracts respecting the leases of the premises, purchase and sale of goods, &c., but in no way relating to the promotion of the Company, are always current. These it is impossible to specify, and applicants will be deemed to have waived any obligation there may be to set out particulars of these, either under Section 38 of the Companies Act, 1867, or otherwise.

The only other Contracts which have been entered into, are:—A Contract dated 21st November, 1889, between Charles Digby Harrod, of the on t, and Harrod's Stores Limited of the ot' art, and a Contract dated the 21st November, 1889, between the Company of the one part, and William George Smart of the other part, regarding his appointment as Manager.

Applications for Shares should be made on the accompanying form, and forwarded to The London and County Banking Company, Limited, or their Branches, with a remittance for the amount of the Deposit.

If the whole amount applied for by the applicant be not allotted, the surplus amount paid on deposit will be appropriated towards the sum due on allotment. Where no allotment is made the deposit will be returned in full.

Application will be made for a quotation on the Stock Exchange.

The Memorandum and Articles of Association, the above-mentioned Contract for Sale, the Contract with Mr. Smart, together with the Report of Messrs. Deloitte, Dever, Griffiths & Co., can be inspected at the Offices of the Company's Solicitors.

Prospectuses and Forms of Application can be obtained at the Offices of the Company, or of the Bankers, Brokers and Solicitors.

LONDON, 23rd November, 1889.

was worth more than £7 per week. Ironically during Burbidge's term of office, Harrods surpassed Whiteleys as the largest store in London and in the world.

Charles Digby Harrod was able to retire for good and for the next fifteen years enjoyed village life first in Somerset and then Sussex, where he died in 1905 at the age of sixty-four.

Richard Burbidge was born in 1847, the fourth son of George Bishop Burbidge, a Bulkington farmer. He went to school in Devizes and Melksham. When his father died in 1861 he moved to London as an apprentice to Mr Jonathon Puckridge, whose business was provisions, grocery and wine merchant. His shop was on the site subsequently occupied by Bourne and Hollingsworth.

Richard Burbidge remained there for five years before

moving on to start in business on his own account. However, he seems to have preferred to work in larger concerns and after a spell in South Kensington he moved to become General Superintendent of the recently opened Army and Navy Auxiliary.

His next move was to Whiteley's of Westbourne Grove where he became manager of the provisions section and where he stayed for eight-and-a-half years. His final position before joining Harrods was as manager of the West Kensington Stores where he remained for two years. He joined Harrods as general manager and subsequently held the position of managing director.

Burbidge was married in 1868 to Emily Woodman of Melksham. Together they had two sons and four daughters. The eldest son was Sir Woodman Burbidge who joined Harrods on 4 December 1893 and became managing director on 27 June 1917, following his father's death. His second son Mr Herbert Burbidge became a director of Hudsons Bay Company. His first wife, Emily, died in 1905 and in 1910 he married his second wife, Lilian Burbidge, the youngest daughter of Mr J. A. Preece of Herefordshire.

If the latter Harrod had driven himself hard, then Richard Burbidge drove himself harder; he worked from 7.00 a.m. until well into the night and the hours of business were extremely long at the time he went into the store. Sir Alfred Newton, Bt, Chairman of the directors of Harrods wrote of him:

'I have been asked the secret of Richard Burbidge's success. In my judgement his untiring industry takes the first place. He knew no hours, often commencing the day's labours at five o'clock and finishing only when the day's work was over.'

Writing just after Burbidge's death in 1917, one of his contemporaries pointed out that pure financial success was only part of the story:

'The memorable matter, however, is not that Sir Richard built up a vast organization, but rather the way in which his success was achieved. When he took over the management of Harrods the shop day began at seven in the morning and ended at nine o'clock in the evening, except on Fridays and Saturdays, when the closing hours were ten and eleven respectively. It often happened, indeed, that messengers were not released from duty until after midnight on Saturday, or well into Sunday morning. Although these exhausting hours were sanctioned by usage, one of Sir Richard Burbidge's first acts on taking over the reins of Harrods business was to effect a substantial improvement, and that policy of consideration for his employees he pursued progressively throughout. Still a pioneer in the interests of shop assistants, a further act on their behalf, as well as on that of the shopping public, was to bring the business day at Harrods to a close at six o'clock. Harrods, moreover, were the first to close one day in the week at one o'clock, this rule being instituted long before the Shops Act came into force.'

Certainly his hard work paid financial dividends and the growth in profits is shown in the company's annual results. The financial year ended on 31 December and subsequently on 31 January, and over a twenty year period looked like this:

31 December 1890 £12,479
31 December 1895 £51,076
31 January 1900 (financial year changed)
                  £84,228
31 January 1905 £135,266
31 January 1910 £210,092

That period saw the staff numbers multiply to thousands and the size of the building increased at a pace to match. England was enjoying a period of prosperity and Harrods' fortunes reflected that buoyant mood. However, the skill and dedication of Burbidge's direction were very much instrumental in the upward surge of the store and it would be wrong to put all the credit for the boom in business down to national economic conditions.

He it was who purchased for staff recreational purposes

Mill Lodge at Barnes, a fine old country house set in four-teen acres of grounds, and that facility still exists today. He was also responsible for Harrods' furniture depository, built nearby on the Thames in 1894.

At Knightsbridge there was also much activity. To be precise even the stairs were no longer standing still. In 1898 Harrods introduced to an amazed public the first moving staircase in London. It was not an escalator as we know it today for there were no steps but it was very much the forerunner of today's escalators. It was merely a con-veyor belt tilted at a slight angle to travel upwards in a gentle incline. Nevertheless, it excited much press com-ment at the time. The *Pall Mall Gazette* had this to say: 'Such a getting upstairs there was yesterday as has not been hitherto attempted in this country. The novelty consists in an adaptation of the magic carpet of the fairy tale to the prosaic purposes of stairs. Thus, you do not so much get upstairs as you get upstairs by the stairs going up with you ... When you have reached the height you desire, the "Moving Staircase" is warranted to unload you without inconvenience to itself or danger to yourself.'

The *Daily Chronicle* wrote: 'The operation is simplicity itself. The "traveller" puts his feet on the moving staircase, his hand on the rail and is "wafted" by imperceptible motion to the place where he would be.'

The site for this escalator was in the area later occupied by the great banking hall and now the perfumery depart-ment; a nice Harrodian touch was the provision of an attendant at the top to administer sal volatile or cognac to anyone unnerved by the ride.

By this time Richard Burbidge had conceived the idea of Harrods occupying the whole of the island site that is the store we know today. However, there were at that time not a few problems between him and the fulfilment of that dream. To start with, there were still a number of private residences and some commercial concerns on the site. As always the freehold to public houses was parti-cularly difficult to come by and there were two. One was

The Buttercup which was half way along today's front of the store and the other, The Friend in Hand, was at the back where the Man's Shop now adjoins the Hans Road receiving bank.

The development of the site is a fascinating story in its own right. An early record of the area exists, dated 1780, the diagram (see page 24) is taken from a print which hangs in the managing director's office. By 1850 the picture had changed somewhat and a diagram of the area shows some familiar landmarks. Hans Road is marked and at the other end of the building is New Street, now Hans Crescent. The street at the rear of the block called Upper North Street looks as if it ran where Basil Street runs but that is an illusion. Basil Street in fact runs through the block of houses between Upper North Street and Exeter Place. The two shaded squares mark the area occupied by Henry Harrod's shop.

Following the fire in December 1883, the store was rebuilt and the extent of the premises is shown in diagram (iii). Gradually the store grew until by 1894 it occupied the area marked in diagram (iv).

At this time the block behind the store was demolished and Basil Street was born as shown in diagram (v).

By the turn of the century the position shown in diagram (vi) had been reached and shortly afterwards work commenced on rebuilding the front of the store. John Allen and Sons of Kilburn were the contractors and they built to a design by the architect C. W. Stephens. Stephens was also responsible for Claridges and had worked on the nearby store, Harvey Nichols. Diagram (vii) shows the progress of the work on the front of the store.

Significant extra purchases were made in 1902 as shown in diagram (viii) but it was not until 1911 (diagram ix) that the full island site as we know it today was acquired.

The famous terracotta of the façade was commissioned by Richard Burbidge and was supplied by Doultons, who also provided the tiling for the meat halls, the designs for which they in turn commissioned from W. J. Neatby. The

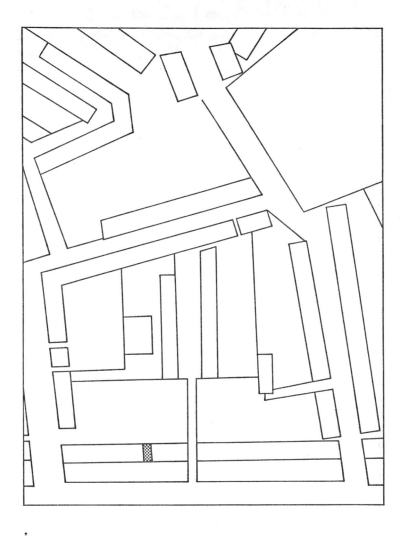

i
1780

ii
1850

iii
1884

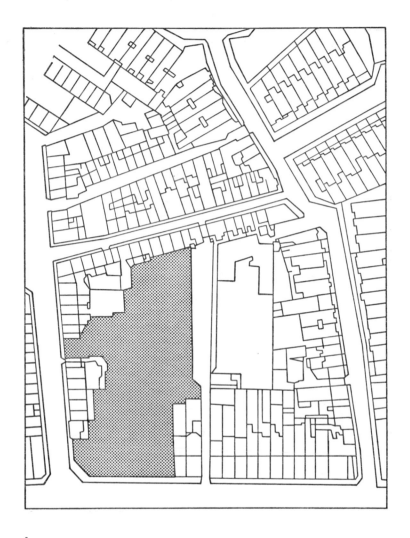

iv
1894

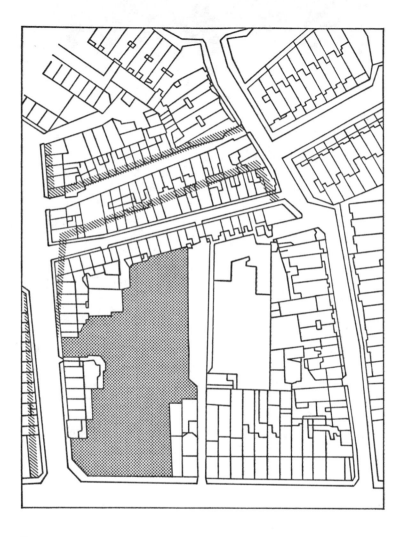

v

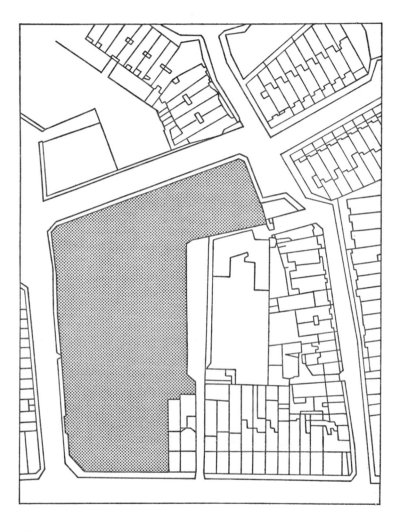

vi
1900–1

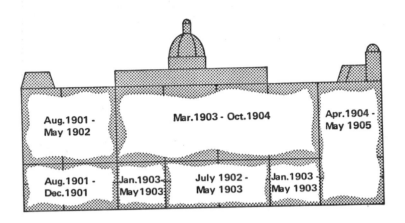

vii

interior shopfitting work was done largely by the firm of
Frederick Sage Limited. Indeed it appears from their company records that the work on Harrods occupied the entire
staff of Sage for the first five years of the twentieth century.

A souvenir booklet entitled 'The House That Every
Woman Knows' was produced for the Diamond Jubilee of
the firm in 1909 and explains the operation on the front
elevation:

'... the policy being to reconstruct a complete block with
an area of 120 feet by 200 feet each summer so that the
business might suffer as little inconvenience as possible
from the operations. Thus each year the premises grew
with mechanical regularity until the gigantic fabric which
is now so much admired by architectural students was completed.

In connection with this rebuilding a remarkable record
was achieved which has probably never before nor since
been equalled.

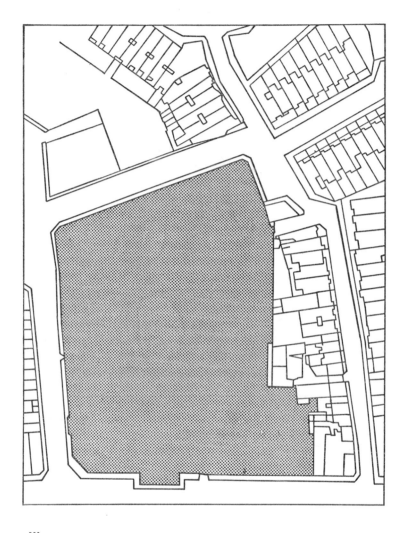

viii
1902

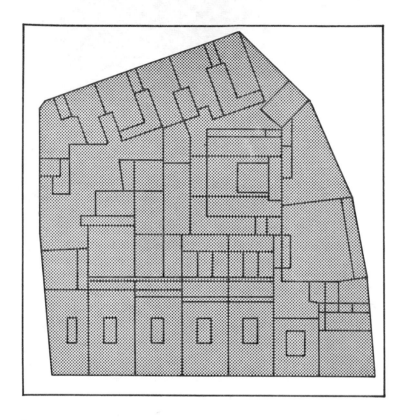

ix
1911

The final and most westerly block, measuring 80 feet by 120 feet, was actually demolished and rebuilt between 27 April and 4 June, a period of less than six weeks ...'

As the building had grown so had the business. By the turn of the century Harrods was the premiere and largest department store in London, having wrested that honour from William Whiteley's. The range of merchandise stocked was by now formidable and catalogues that survive from that time are testimony to the fact that Harrods thoroughly earned the telegraphic address 'Everything London' which it still retains. What is perhaps even more striking today are the prices; from the 1904 catalogue I give three examples (pages 34 and 35).

Meanwhile on the international scene at the turn of the century the Boer War held the spotlight. Sir Alfred Newton, Bt, the chairman, was Lord Mayor of London in 1899 and it fell to him to make the appeal which led to the rapid raising and equipping of the City Imperial Volunteers. His son, Harry, and Burbidge's son, Woodman, who had by this time joined the store's management team, were largely instrumental in obtaining the equipment and they leaned heavily on the store's resources to do so. Even after they had embarked for South Africa Burbidge's diary contained entries such as:

'Order for 1,600 helmets for CIV ... packing 100 sets of mule harness ... 100 more saddles for CIV ...' and when the CIV returned in October 1900 he noted that 1,250 luncheon packages were sent down to Southampton by pantechnicon.

The year 1911 was something of a landmark in the history of Harrods, as it was the year during which the full island site that Harrods now occupies was finally acquired. By happy coincidence, it was also the year of the coronation of King George V and a souvenir brochure printed by the store at that time starts 'His Most Gracious Majesty's memorable words, "Wake up England" have not been forgotten by his people, and Harrods today presents a striking example of what can be done by British Capital and British

TABLE D'HOTE DINNER,

3/6 FROM 6.30 TO 9.0 O'CLOCK. **3/6**

SATURDAYS AND SUNDAYS EXCEPTED.

MENU.

Hors D'œuvres Varie.

Consomme Chiffonade.
Thick Mock Turtle.

Turbot, Lobster Sauce.
Fried Smelts, Sauce Tartar.

Mutton Cutlets, Provenciale.
Braized Partridge, Chasseur.

Roast Sirloin Beef.
Boiled Turkey, Celery Sauce.
Spinach.   Sauté Potatoes.

Victoria Pudding.
Custard Fritters.

Cheese Fondu.

Dessert.

Steak, Beef	...	...	...	0/11	0/10
,,	Buttock	...	...	1/0	0/11
,,	Rump ...	...	...	1/3	1/2
,,	Fillet ...	...	1/3½	1/3	1/3½
Sirloin, whole...	...	...	0/10½	0/9
,,	prime cut	...	...	0/11½	0/10½
Gravy Beef	...	...	...	0/8	0/7
Soup Meat	...	...	...	0/6½	0/6
Ox Kidneys	...	...	...	0/11
Suet ...	...	...	...	0/8
Sausages	...	...	...	0/5
Pieces, from	...	...	...	0/8

Notice.—Kidneys, Sweetbreads, etc., do not travel well during the warm weather, and can only be sent at customer's own risk.

Labour combined with British Enterprise.' And Harrods Limited was twenty-one years old.

The brochure featured a picture of the store complete with an artist's impression of a two hundred foot tower that was to be built to commemorate the coronation. In the event it never materialized; residents opposite raised objections and the project had to be shelved. Soon the country had entered much harder economic times and the post war era saw the idea abandoned, but the legacy of the plan lives on in the form of the gigantic foundations of the arch that affords access to the Hans Road receiving bank at the back of the store. A stone commemorates the laying of the tower's foundation by Richard Burbidge on 13 September 1911.

1913 saw Harrods receive a Royal Warrant from Queen Mary. She was not the only member of the royal family to shop at the store; Queen Alexandra, Edward VII's widow, was a regular customer and the last Czar of Russia's children also made an expedition, recalled by a member of the staff of that time:

'They each were bought sailor suits.' Photographs of them during the last years of the Czar's reign frequently feature them in those sailor suits.

The same member of staff married a young man who had joined Harrods from the Clapham Stores as a protégé of William Kibble; his name was William Miln and he subsequently became the food hall manager in succession to Kibble. Mrs Miln also recalls that then ladies did not shop in the afternoon; perhaps some housekeepers and American tourists did but ladies only came in the afternoon to take tea in the restaurant.

In 1914 came the Great War and once more the formidable resources of the store were mobilized, this time to supply and equip hospitals and other necessities for the men in the trenches of France. Harrods suffered its share of losses. On the first landing of one of the staircases is a list of the 147 staff members who gave their lives. At one time, in 1916, Harrods had 2,000 of its staff on war service. This led to a shortage of men in the shop and women filled many posts that were traditionally male preserves; a particular example was the use of women as 'Green men'.

The store itself felt the effects of war and Mr William Miln, the food section manager, had to introduce food rationing. Harrods did this quite unilaterally and in advance of the government scheme. The booklet informing customers of the details is shown overleaf.

Richard Burbidge continued to work tirelessly for the company and was rewarded in 1916 by a baronetcy. However, the pace he set himself had taken its toll and he did not survive the war. On 31 May 1917 he died from a heart attack.

The term of office of Sir Richard Burbidge was, without doubt, the period that made Harrods the most famous department store in the world. It would be unrealistic to attribute all the credit to one man; but he was in charge of a staff which numbered 6,000 at the time of his death (interestingly 1,000 more regular staff than today's number) and all of them played a part in the development; also it was a time when economic and social developments facilitated the expansion. Nevertheless, there is no doubt that the energy and drive of Sir Richard were quite remarkable and that he was a very thoughtful man with much concern for the welfare of his staff, who repaid him with great loyalty. There are still pensioners of Harrods who remember him warmly. The following is an extract from the minutes of the board meeting held on 6 June 1917.

It was resolved to record the directors' very high appreciation of his uprightness of character and outstanding commercial ability during his many years with the company. He joined the company on 25 March 1891. Under his managing directorship the trade has enormously expanded until it now reaches to all parts of the world, while during this period the annual profit has increased from £16,071 to £309,227 before the war. The staff has increased from 200 to 6,000, and the hours of employment have been substantially reduced and the working conditions improved all round. His was an attractive and

HARRODS INTRODUCE RATIONS

We must look upon things as they are, not as we would wish them to be.—Napoleon.

AN URGENT MESSAGE TO HARRODS CUSTOMERS

So far as supplies permit Harrods will ration their customers equally from Monday, Jan 21

OUR POLICY AND METHOD

Doubly desirous as we are in these days of ensuring 'the greatest good of the greatest number' we have decided, after the most earnest consideration, to begin on Monday, January 21st, the 'rationing' of essential Foodstuffs, limiting the supply of each and every rationed article to only such customers as have hitherto regularly purchased these same articles at Harrods. We shall begin with

MEAT
MARGARINE
BUTTER

Subject always to Government Regulation the Meat ration will be 2 lbs. per head per week and the Margarine or Butter ration 4 ozs. per head per week, these being the suggested 'voluntary' rations.

The ration for Sugar is of course already fixed.

FILL IN THE FORM OVERLEAF

If you have been a regular purchaser of Meat, Margarine or Butter at Harrods and wish to continue to obtain supplies of any or all of these articles on the new 'rationed' basis, please fill in the Registration Form on the back, and bring or send it to The Manager of Harrods Food Bureau, Harrods Ltd, London, SW 1, not later than Tuesday, January 15th.

Unless a customer registers by means of this Form Harrods cannot undertake to supply him or her with any Meat, Margarine or Butter.

As the Registrations are completed a further communication will be sent you.

REGISTRATION FORM

The Head of the Household should fill this in and return it to Harrods Food Bureau by TUESDAY, JANUARY 15th

I HEREBY declare that I have been a regular customer of Harrods for

MEAT MARGARINE BUTTER

(Cross out any item to which the statement does not apply)

and I am desirous of continuing to obtain, through Harrods, 'rationed' supplies of

MEAT MARGARINE BUTTER

(Cross out the articles not required)

and further I undertake, subject to my being registered for supplies of such article (or articles) at Harrods that I will not register elsewhere for the supply of such article or articles.

*Name in full*_____
Write clearly, stating Mr., Mrs. or Miss

*Give regular number to be provided for*_____

*Address in full*_____

_____

If you are an account customer } _____
please give number of your account }

If you obtain your sugar through Harrods } _____
give Pink number on your Old card }

HARRODS Ld   Woodman Burbidge
Managing Director   LONDON SW 1

charming personality; he endeared himself to all with whom he came into daily contact. His loss will be felt not only in Harrods but in wider circles outside.

He was succeeded by his son, Sir Woodman Burbidge, Bt, who faced the unenviable task of following a great father at a time when the country faced economic and social instability. Nevertheless Sir Woodman determined to lead Harrods to further heights and one major project that he undertook was the completion of a new despatch area at Trevor Square. It was obviously desirable for the two buildings to be connected and to this end a network of tunnels started in his father's day was completed in 1921. Harrods underground was, and is, a fascinating place, a veritable labyrinth of passages and storage areas, named according to the place to which they provide access; for example 'Frosty Way' leads to the refrigeration rooms. It is as well for new recruits that the underground streets are named for if it is easy to get lost in the store it is considerably easier to get lost underneath it where there are no directions and no daylight. Right up to the early 1970s the cash tube room was down there and this was where twenty cashiers sat at the end of thirty-nine miles of tubes and waited for a carrier, drawn by the vigorous suction, to arrive. When it came it was opened, the contents checked, the appropriate change inserted and then the carrier was popped back into the tube to make the return journey to its department of origin. That department might have been up to a quarter of a mile away; in fact the longest 'tube journey' was fifty-four seconds covered at a speed of seventeen miles per hour. Ultimately the sheer pressure of workload began to be too much for the system installed by Sir Woodman, and nowadays Harrods is served by on-the-spot cash registers. Perhaps another reason it was changed relates to the mid-1960s when one of the temporary staff was coping very well with the Christmas rush considering her lack of experience. She sold an item worth £64, a very substantial purchase. The customer was an Arab gentleman, then far less of an everyday occurrence than today. And he handed her sixty-four one pound notes. That was six weeks wages to her! She put the money straight down the tube without placing it in a carrier. The unsuspecting cashiers were churning through the day's work in the tube room when all of a sudden the tubehead flew open and unleashed a ticker tape bombardment of sixty-four shredded one pound notes.

There is still a message tube system operating in the store for internal mail.

Although the years between the wars were lean times for the country and the store, Harrods battled on spurred not least by a wager that Woodman Burbidge, then on the management board, had struck with another shopkeeper of the time. The bet was laid on 4 January 1917 and read:

Wagered Mr Woodman Burbidge that within six (6) years of the declaration of peace we would overtake and pass Harrods Limited in annual returns. The stake is to be a silver miniature replica of the loser's store.
H. Gordon Selfridge.

In 1927, eight years after the official ending of the war, Sir Woodman wrote to Gordon Selfridge to point out to him that Selfridges had not drawn level, far less passed Harrods and reminded him of the bet. He requested that the silver replica should be of Harrods rather than of Selfridges and Selfridge gracefully agreed.

This was a typical example of the good natured rivalry that characterized the relationship between the two leading stores of the day; it was a relationship that set the pattern for future generations and to this day the feeling between the two superstores is competitive but cordial. From the fact that Selfridge did not seek a rematch we may deduce, perhaps, that he knew when he was beaten; Harrods remains substantially ahead fifty years later.

Sir Woodman Burbidge was concerned with turning more and more of the building into selling space. Whilst the store achieved its present external dimensions in 1911 and apart from some work on the façade, notably at the rear of the building, it has changed little since and the interior work has been continuously developed and changed, excepting for a period during the Second World War.

In 1911 the area covered by the building was far too large for the trade that the store could hope to achieve and in order to derive some income from the extra space considerable room was let as flats.

Sir Woodman started the process of taking over the flats and turning them into selling departments. It was not without its problems. In 1928 work had to be suspended for a year due to the depressed economic conditions and when it was resumed a year later a structural snag was met. An iron stanchion collapsed in the south west corner of the store and hydraulic jacks had to be inserted to gradually raise the surrounding area to allow more solid foundations to be built.

Sir Woodman's drive and energy were not to be denied, and his last major project before the Second World War was the new escalators. His father's moving staircase had passed its day and no longer existed in the area that was now the great Banking Hall. The two ways of getting to the floors above ground level were by the stairs or in the lifts but Sir Woodman resolved to end this state of affairs and the escalators that serve the store today were designed and built.

And so Harrods moved through the inter-war period of 1918 to 1939; as always the trends of the day were reflected in this most fashion-conscious of businesses and in the era of jazz and the Charleston, of Fred Astaire and Ginger Rogers, tea dances were a regular feature in the Georgian restaurant. Here it was that a young man took the first tentative steps that blossomed into a career which made him famous the world over as the king of strict tempo dancing, Victor Sylvester.

Sir Woodman's son, Richard, following in the family tradition was appointed general manager in 1928. In 1935

he became managing director while Sir Woodman remained as chairman of the board.

In 1939 came the Second World War and Harrods provided its share of people for the armed forces. The company's war service books runs to 1,800 names and its
detachment of special constables was the largest of any
retail house in London. Business naturally declined and
by the latter years of the war was severely reduced.

The building with its own power and water supplies was
an obvious choice for use by the forces and both the Royal
Navy and the Canadian Air Force took over parts of it. In
the basement the roof was strengthened in one area so that
it could serve as an air raid shelter; a first aid post was
prepared including the conversion of a Harrods van to an
ambulance.

Air raid precautions had been undertaken shortly before
the official outbreak of war and the story survives of an
occasion when these preparations were to be inspected by
the officer in charge of ARP for the area.

The Banking Hall was used to stage a demonstration of
first aid facilities and the inspection team was then due to
move out to the then new escalator hall by Door 5. Wishing
to put on an impressive and realistic display Harrods had
arranged to stage a simulated explosion in this area. Sound
effects were provided by some staff out of sight on the first
floor landing with an assortment of iron sheets and metal
dustbins filled with nuts and bolts; visual effects consisted
of two arc lamps semi-concealed in the two small rooms on
either side of Door 5.

The entourage walked from the Banking Hall to the
escalator hall to be met by this mock explosion. Clearly it
was not mock enough for, with a few startled exclamations,
the inspecting team bolted back into the Banking Hall
in fear of their lives, convinced that the real war had
begun.

The exterior of the building escaped any serious damage
from the bombing although the famous dome and parts of
the west end of the store were affected and not finally put

right until the 1950s. On the other side of Brompton Road
the premises used by Harrods Estate Offices were demolished by a flying bomb.

Throughout the war fire pickets were on duty at Harrods, with staff working on a rota basis and sleeping both
in the basement and in the Georgian restaurant. The
fashion workrooms were extended and devoted to the
making of uniforms. Parachutes and aircraft parts were also
manufactured inside the building.

Sir Woodman Burbidge died in 1945 and his son Sir
Richard succeeded him as chairman of the board and
began the task of re-establishing trade in the difficult years
following the ending of the war.

One hundred years is something of a milestone for a
business and Harrods could look back on a century of
success in 1949. A model of the original shop was built and
housed in the Central Display Hall. The trade had been
£20 per week in 1849 and increased to around £20,000,000
for the group in 1949.

The continental *Daily Mail* printed a *Centenary
Souvenir of Harrods* on Saturday, 30 April 1949 and a
column of facts and figures makes fascinating reading:

'Share capital amounts to £6,500,000 authorized and
£6,215,194 issued and fully paid.
General reserve, £500,000; contingencies reserve £419,191;
buildings reserve £419,032.
Bank: customer's balances £1,846,929.
Stockholders number, 30,000. Stockholders of not more
than £200 of stock, 23,000.
Insurance value of properties of group, £12,000,000.
Insurance value of fixtures of group £4,000,000.
Estate office, properties sold (1946) £3,500,000.
Auction galleries sales (1946), £336,000.
Customers' furs in storage of group, £475,000.
Record day's trading Harrods sale (pre-war) £250,000.
Record week's trading Harrods sale (pre-war) £550,000.

Clothing and points coupons received in a year, £14,500,000.

Export trade per annum, £200,000.

Floor area, Harrods (including warehouses) 35 acres.

String used in a year, 8,000 miles.

Removals warehouse space, 3,500,000 sq. ft.

Letters despatched in a day, 6,000.

Store carpet runners, $2\frac{1}{4}$ miles.

Library books lent in a year, 1,000,000.

Telephone calls in a year, 1,250,000.

Total staff of Group including factories, 9,500.

Salaries, wages and pensions of group excluding factories, £2,119,000.

Electricity units generated by Harrods plant, yearly total, pre-war, 9,250,000.

Staff restaurant meals per day, Harrods store 8,000.'

The same publication draws to our attention the enormous range of Harrods factories and workrooms. From the millinery workshop 'where dozens of highly skilled girls are employed' to the fur-cleaning and fur-modelling shop where 'apart from the "Harrodizing" process of scientifically cleaning and rejuvenating furs, and remodelling old fur coats to a later style, a considerable activity goes on, creating from new skins the loveliest of garments ...' Then there were the tailoring workrooms, the floral workroom, workshops for clock repairs, making medical preparations, a printing plant 'for relief stamping of stationery, copperplate engraving, letterpress printing, bookbinding and the making of special office books ...', a shoe factory, a leather goods factory, a silver plate workshop, a cardboard box factory, a piano factory, a casemaking workshop, a confectionery factory, a bakery and many others.

During its first hundred years Harrods had made some valuable acquisitions. In 1913, the young Sir Woodman travelled to South America where he became captivated with the idea of a second Harrods in Buenos Aires. That year Harrods (Buenos Aires) was founded and it is the only other store that has ever been allowed to use the Harrods name. There are, of course, other shops called Harrods but they take their name from their owners and are not part of the group. Travellers to Buenos Aires say the store there is a fine building. It was sold so that the link is no longer maintained. Harrods (Buenos Aires) still exists and continues to trade as Harrods.

In 1914, Harrods acquired Dickins and Jones Ltd of Regent Street. It is still part of the Harrods group today and has two satellites, one in Richmond and one opening at Milton Keynes in the autumn of 1981. In 1919, Harrods interests spread to the north and Kendal Milne of Manchester was taken over. It is now part of the House of Fraser Midland group. D. H. Evans came next in 1928, and was the company's first Oxford Street store. Like Dickins and Jones it is still part of the Harrods group and in 1980 it gained a sister store in the new Wood Green shopping centre.

The expansion continued and further acquisitions were made; John Walsh of Sheffield, now called Binns, J. F. Rockhey of Torquay, now called Dingles, Rackhams of Birmingham, since rebuilt and now part of the House of Fraser Midland group, and Hendersons of Liverpool, now called Binns.

With the famous Knightsbridge store as its flagship this was a most desirable group and as the 1950s drew towards a close they brought the end of the era of the Burbidges with Hugh Fraser's acquisition of the Harrods group. The Burbidges had run Harrods for sixty years.

Improvements in working conditions came under the first Sir Richard long before they were forced upon him by law and this concern for staff was also a feature of his son, Sir Woodman's, style of management. Perhaps more than either of them, however, the younger Sir Richard possessed the ability to bring a human touch to the business of leading 5,000 employees. His chauffeur worked on in Harrods for twenty years after the takeover but could still remember Sir Richard's habit of sitting in the front seat and chatting:

'He used to come down to the despatch office and wish us a happy Christmas; there would be over a hundred men there and he would know every one of them by name.'

Sir Richard's ability to know his staff by name was legendary. 'He used to see us all before we went on holiday, you know,' recalls one of the management team who served under him. 'You only began to relax and feel you were on holiday after he had seen you to sign you off.'

The new owner, Hugh Fraser, was a man of immense energy and drive and was determined that Harrods should go from strength to strength under the Fraser flag. Born in Glasgow in 1903, he became managing director of the family firm (by coincidence started in 1849) at the tender age of twenty-one and during the twenties and thirties, whilst most retailers were struggling, he threw himself into expanding the premises and business. 'I am tired of hearing people talk about the depression in trade. If I were not convinced of Glasgow's future I would never contemplate extending on the scale mapped out,' he said.

Business flourished to the point where in 1948 Fraser's became a public company. He was amongst the first to use the leapfrogging tactic of releasing the capital tied up in one building to buy the next. Those financing him were prepared to approve plans as long as they could see a safe return on their investment and he always managed to show a sound enough profit.

It was this system that enabled Fraser's to make a £3 million bid for the Scottish Drapery Corporation in July 1952 when his company's balance sheet the previous January had shown a cash balance of £7,000 and net surplus assets of £229,000. He knew that the SDC accounts showed the value of the properties to be £2.3 million, based on 1947 figures and that they were worth nearer to £4.5 million. It was the revaluation of these properties and the sale and lease-back tactic that enabled him to raise the money to bid for his next target, Binns. It was also the first time he met with serious resistance in a take-over and it was only after a considerable battle that he won. Hugh Fraser's first foray into the West End of London was the acquisition of John Barkers, Derry & Toms and Pontings. This came in the summer of 1957 and was the forerunner of his most famous take-over, Harrods.

The 1959 battle to gain control of Harrods is part of the legend of the City of London and the Stock Exchange; it captured the imagination of the general public and the interest with which it was followed and the depth in which it was reported in the national press indicates the place Harrods holds in the affections of the nation.

Harrods was vulnerable to a take-over bid from the moment in 1958 when it became known that the company's properties had been revalued at £20 million on an issued capital of £8 million. Burbidge was naturally as aware of this as anyone else and made overtures in the direction of the Debenham group, who were at that time comfortably the largest store group in the country. It was inevitable, therefore, that when Hugh Fraser first entered the field in earnest he found the Harrods board favouring the Debenhams link.

At that time the resources of the House of Fraser were in fact very little larger than those of Harrods; Fraser and Harrods put together were not as big as Debenhams. The figures were:

Debenhams	£56 million
Harrods	£23 million
House of Fraser	£28 million

However, Hugh Fraser threw himself into the battle with his customary verve and determination. Drama was injected into the affair when a third contender declared himself in the form of Joseph Collier of United Drapery Stores. Hugh Fraser always regarded Collier as a more dangerous counter-bidder than Debenhams since Collier had good connections in the insurance world and UDS was being backed in its attempt to buy Harrods by the Eagle Star Group.

Debenham's offer was worth £34,500,000 and Collier's approximately £36,000,000. Both had the edge of Hugh Fraser's first offer of £32,600,000 but he soon responded with more favourable terms and a letter declaring his resolve to maintain the traditions of Harrods and setting out the record of his company.

Collier was the first to withdraw saying that he had no intention of destroying himself to get control of Harrods. It is thought he offered his 500,000 preference shares to John Bedford, the chairman of Debenhams, and that Bedford declined at the price. Whether that is true or not, it is certain that Hugh Fraser made a trip to see Joseph Collier and came away with the shares.

All these comings and goings were recorded in the press and a French newspaper remarked at the time: 'This financial battle ... is being followed by the English with the same interest which they normally reserve for the sports results.'

The two offers seem to have been fairly evenly matched in the end but it appears that the Fraser campaign was carried out with more thoroughness and determination and Debenhams eventually conceded defeat on Monday, 24 August. David had felled Goliath and in September 1959, Hugh Fraser went to London to preside over his first board meeting as Harrods' chairman. A new era had begun.

So now the store was into the swinging sixties and the new managing director, Alfred Spence, was confronted by a challenge as demanding as any faced by his predecessors. He had the job of seeing Harrods into the House of Fraser group. Aleck Craddock who served under him as section manager of the food halls and later as director of administration recalls that Alfred Spence 'was a warm man with a great deal of the flair for staff relationships that had earlier been shown by the Burbidges. He was able in his years as managing director to convert the doubters and the sceptics from the old dynasty to acceptance of the new.'

Alfred Spence was conscious of the criticism that long-standing customers would heap on a new management that did not remain faithful to the traditions of Harrods. His management style was accordingly cautious but it was also sound and the store went through the sixties with its finances and reputation intact. The major innovation of this period was the opening of Way In. It was the era of Carnaby Street and the boutique and for the first time Harrods customers winced under the onslaught of piped music and flashing lights. The new chairman, Sir Hugh Fraser, who had succeeded his father, Lord Fraser of Allender, on the latter's death in 1966, took a particular interest in the Way In project; it was the first of many occasions when he backed the investment of large sums of money to develop and update Harrods.

And so the store reached 1970, an eventful and fateful year in its history. In March Alfred Spence died and was succeeded as managing director by Gordon Anthony. Gordon Anthony had given a lifetime of service to Harrods, as had his father before him, and as merchandise director he was the natural choice for managing director. But fate intervened and sadly within two months he was dead also.

The shock of two such changes in so short a time affected the morale of the store. By 1970, the annual trade was around the £27,000,000 mark. Inflation was beginning to have an effect and the capital cost of much needed re-development of the store was rising ever faster. Overheads needed tight control on a monthly basis and the increased cost of living caused the 5,000 staff to look to the company for substantial pay rises.

In June Robert Midgley was appointed managing director. Trusting in Lord Fraser's adage that 'turnover takes care of most things in retail' Robert Midgley brought about a revolution in the sedate ways of the Knightsbridge emporium, with a view to gaining an immediate improvement in the annual trade. What he achieved in the ten years he was managing director speaks for itself. The sales figure for the year ending 31 January 1970 was £26,477,000. The sales figure for the year ending 31 January 1980 was £145,000,000.

A considerable amount of that increase can be put down to inflation but the whole story is far more ambitious. Harrods today is a very different place to the rather quaint, dated store that Robert Midgley inherited in 1970. He set new standards of 'housekeeping', based on the simple premise that the retailer's job is to display merchandise in such a way as to catch the attention of anyone who passes and then be there and be awake when someone does stop to look at it. Harrods buyers were powerfully reminded that their flair as buyers was liable to founder unless display was good enough. As a great believer in what he calls 'management on the hoof' he frequently went around the whole thirty-five acres of the store and warehouses two or three times a day. It soon became known that if he issued an instruction he would be back twenty minutes later to assess progress. Although this was not always appreciated at first, it was a discipline that Harrods sorely needed at that time and his management team was gradually won over when the results of his driving energy brought increased business.

All successful men need a little luck and Robert Midgley had his in the form of a tourist boom in the mid seventies. That the store was in a position to cash in on the boom was in no small measure due to his early efforts to smarten up everything about the place and to shake out the dust.

Hard as he might push his management there is a limit to what can be achieved with antiquated departments and fixtures and he embarked upon a programme of modernization and refurbishing.

The first area to benefit was the food halls, appropriately enough as Harrods started as a grocer's shop. The pantry and dairy produce departments emerged with a much greater emphasis on self-selection. Not only was this dictated by the ever increasing cost, and shortage in supply of manpower to staff the area but it was increasingly being demanded by the shopping habits of the nation. The floral hall and the fruit and vegetable department followed on. It soon became apparent that the alterations were having a beneficial effect on trade, such as could not have been achieved with the old layout.

Next came the great Banking Hall in the centre of the ground floor which could no longer be afforded. Here was conceived and built what must surely be the ultimate perfumery department. Designed by Copeland, Novak and Israel of New York, it consisted of an archipelago of counters set in a sea of real marble, quarried in Italy especially for Harrods, and cushioned with red velvet.

The support and encouragement of the chairman, Sir Hugh Fraser, was an important factor in these developments, as was illustrated at a dinner.

The buyers invite personalities to come and speak to them as a group on occasion and one well respected figure from the retail world gave as the gist of his speech the fact that the shape of retailing would alter considerably over the coming years, in particular it would be influenced by the arrival of the hypermarket, which could sound the death knell of the department store. When asked how he accounted for Harrods' undoubted boom, the respected speaker answered that department stores were enjoying a 'tail wind' during the build up of the storm but that when the hurricane struck they would be swept away defenceless.

Throughout the exchange Robert Midgley sat expressionless and inscrutable (a sure sign that he disapproves). Several months later he rose to make his speech at the annual dinner given by Sir Hugh for the Harrods buyers and managers. Traditionally this is a time when Robert Midgley shares his thinking on future trading patterns. He related for Sir Hugh's benefit the 'tail wind' theory and then added, 'What this gentleman seems not to have realized is the quarter from which Harrods' own particular "tail wind" is blowing.' His gaze came to rest on the young chairman. It was an apt acknowledgement by Robert Midgley of Sir Hugh Fraser's contribution. Sir Hugh took a close and continuing interest in all of Robert Midgley's ventures; nobody was, and is, more determined than he that Harrods should be the finest department store in the world and he repeatedly put his company's money and faith behind what he thought were sound ideas.

Many improvements followed; the restaurants brought up to date, the paperback book department was expanded and refitted. the china department was enlarged and new display cabinets installed, the fashion floor was opened up and refitted – and there can surely be no more sumptuous department in the world than Harrods' fur salon.

The two hot summers in 1975 and 1976 heated up staff and customers alike and the chief engineer was despatched to the United States to research air conditioning systems.

If Robert Midgley's good luck was to govern Harrods during a tourist boom then his bad luck was that it was also the time when the urban terrorist became a reality for us all. On the afternoon of Saturday, 21 December 1974 the store was full to overflowing with last minute Christmas shoppers. The staff were gritting their teeth and seasonal ill will and bad temper abounded everywhere . . . a standard run-of-the-mill pre-Christmas Saturday in any department store.

Margaret Fyall was manning her battle station in the house and garden tools department when she noticed a small holdall standing beside one of her fixtures; she told herself it was nothing but a nagging suspicion would not go away and she remembered the message repeatedly circulated by management in the preceding few weeks. She telephoned the security department and Frank Nichols. Harrods' chief security officer, came to investigate. He had dealt with several false alarms already that day but this time a cursory examination told him what he had never wanted to know – that he had a bomb sitting primed and ready to explode in a crowded department store.

He cleared the department and notified the general manager, Aleck Craddock. The fire doors were wound down and the area sealed off. At 5.00 p.m. the bomb exploded and not only the store but the whole of Knightsbridge felt the blast. Aleck Craddock ordered the store to be evacuated; there were no injuries but it had been close and several families who will never know her have reason to be grateful to Margaret Fyall.

Volunteers streamed in unrequested on the Sunday morning to help clear up the wrecked department. Staff who twenty-four hours previously would have happily blown the store and everything in it to eternity, rallied to a man and by evening the area was clear. Rebuilding began at once and the new department was trading again early in 1975.

Robert Midgley always contrived to cut office and administrative space to a minimum in order to make available the greatest possible area for selling and in 1976 he evicted himself and his fellow directors from the beautiful oak panelled suite of offices they occupied on the fourth floor to make room for Olympic Way. This is an unrivalled sports complex, selling the very best and latest equipment and clothing for every imaginable sport. He much enjoys referring to the reclamation of this previously 'unproductive area'.

As the seventies drew to a close Robert Midgley announced his intention to retire as managing director and retain only the chairmanship. He left one major venture unfinished. Like Sir Richard Burbidge, one hundred years before him, Robert Midgley was no great lover of lifts and one of his last major decisions was to approve the installation of a second bank of escalators at the west end of the store.

The achievements of the Midgley decade are apparent and when asked for the most important ingredient in that success his reply is unequivocal: 'Team work; it's a team effort from the most junior Christmas temporary to the most senior manager and everyone has a vital part to play.'

In 1980 Aleck Craddock was appointed managing director. He inherited a fine store and a profitable business but
also a more uncertain economic outlook than any in recent
memory. One thing, however, is certain; no one ever started
in the managing director's office with more goodwill, ad-
miration and affection extended to him by his management
team and staff than did Aleck Craddock.

CHAPTER THREE

The shop floor

The sweet smell of success

Although Harrods started as a grocery store, the perfumery was one of the very earliest additions and dates from 1868. The present department, however, dates from as recently as 1972 when it took over the site previously occupied by the famous Banking Hall. Many people mourned the passing of such a national institution, but it had taken up 11,000 square feet of prime selling space and as the store entered tough economic times in the 1970s it could no longer afford such an extravagant waste of potential.

Retailers tend to divide merchandise and departments into two categories, 'demand' and 'impulse' – those which provide predominantly goods or services which the customer either has to use or at least has a strong intention to buy when entering the store, and those selling predominantly items that customers just happen to see while they are passing and decide to buy on impulse. Naturally, customers *en route* to a demand department should be encouraged to walk through as many impulse departments as possible in the hope that their eyes will alight on something which they decide to buy.

The bank is a demand department and as such belongs in a less prominent position than the perfumery which, whilst having a strong base of demand merchandise, also has a powerful impulse trade. The number of women who have entered the store since 1972 with no immediate intention of buying a lipstick or some eye shadow but who nevertheless went out of the store with some must be legion, but in any event sales have increased in the perfumery hall to such an extent that now it is the top selling department in the store, taking something over £5 million in 1980.

As a spectacle it surpasses any other department of its kind in the world for sumptuousness; the floor is of white marble and the furnishings red velvet. All the major perfumery houses are represented and the consultants wear a distinctive uniform. When a cosmetic house posts a consultant to Harrods it means, quite simply, that she is one of the best they have.

The merchandise ranges from the good quality regular lines of the large American companies like Revlon and Estée Lauder, to the most expensive and exclusive perfumes on the world market.

Why is perfume so expensive? It takes $1\frac{1}{4}$ million roses to make one pound of rose oil. It takes 2 million petals of jasmine to make one pound of jasmine oil – the British yellow jasmine is not as suitable as the French and Chinese flowers which are white and have a more powerful scent. Other typical ingredients are oranges and lemons and herbs such as sweet basil, nutmeg, cloves and coriander. A quality perfume might contain nearly all these ingredients, so the cost is bound to be high on that score alone.

The importance of a new quality perfume to the store can be gauged by the trade it is expected to do. In 1980 Harrods introduced a new perfume by Oscar de la Renta which contained many of those expensive ingredients already mentioned and the target sale for the first six months was £60,000 on that one fragrance alone. In the world of perfume the old adage that 'you get what you pay for' applies as in anything else. Cheap perfume quickly loses its pleasing initial impression and usually leaves the wearer with a cloying sweet smell that is an embarrassment to all downwind.

Perfumes are colour coded from the fresh green fragrances of the light eau de toilettes through the yellow floral perfumes like *Fidji* and *Tramp* to the darker colours which begin with the aldehydes, the most famous of which is perhaps *Chanel Number 5*, and at the far end are the spicy woody scents that usually have Oriental sounding names. Men's colognes and aftershave lotions often fall into this end of the spectrum.

One encouraging trend has been the move away from using whale oil as a fixative, the substance put into a perfume to make it linger on the wearer rather than evaporate quickly. The traditional fixatives were musk, civet and ambergris but the campaign by the wildlife and whale lobbies has been heeded by the cosmetic houses and chemical substitutes are now used in the great majority of cases.

Food, glorious food

In the centre of the ground floor and right at the heart of the store is a section of the business inseparable from the history and tradition of Harrods – the food halls.

The whole area underwent renovation to fixtures and fittings in the early 1970s. There may be some traditionalists who regret the move away from the personal service formerly offered, to the modern approach of self-selection but updating did revitalize trade and enabled Harrods' food halls to continue to compete, with brilliant success, in the decade of the supermarket. By 1980 the sales figures were hovering around the £15 million mark annually.

The Pantry – or grocery department – itself takes approximately twenty per cent of that trade and to do so carries upwards of 15,000 lines; the greater part of the department is devoted to the self service area, just like a superior supermarket, but across from the checkout points is the order section where the Harrods traditions of personal service live on; orders may be placed for gift boxes of champagne and caviar to be sent to the Far East or a pot of yoghurt to be sent round to Kensington.

The Pantry warehouse is on the far side of Brompton Road on the third floor of a building in Trevor Square. The journey involves descending to the basement, navigating a catacomb of tunnels which leads under the Brompton Road and then riding in a freight lift to the stockroom area on the third floor, in all a total distance of over half a mile. Everything sold in the Pantry has to make this journey; the customer who has been left standing in the department with the time honoured words 'I'll just pop over and get one from the stockroom' ringing in her ears may understand the delay in future.

The dairy produce, next door, has a mind boggling selection of cheeses, with separate counters for English and foreign selections, together with a range of creams and yoghurts to satisfy the most discerning of tastes.

Harrods has a reputation for being an expensive store. Its attitude to this is that price is of less concern than value. That is to say, Harrods does not mind its customers saying 'that was expensive' as long as they can truthfully add 'but it was worth every penny'. But it is nice to report that not everything is expensive; Harrods does have particularly competitively priced lines such as own brand butter and bacon.

During the 1970s, as now, Harrods was proud to be an important supplier to the Royal Household at Buckingham Palace, known affectionately as 'Buck House', and the Palace regularly telephones the store to place orders. Newcomers are of course duly appraised of this fact and advised of the passionate desire of the management that this patronage should continue; whilst issuing this instruction the cheese buyer usually contrives to be toying idly with a cheese cutting wire that would sever the head of an ox at a stroke. Obviously impressed by this information was a young lady who had recently joined the dairy produce department as a buyer's clerk. One morning she was diligently pursuing her duties in the office when the telephone rang. It was a very busy morning and the queue of customers had grown to such proportions that the buyer himself was helping out. He was in the midst of a ticklish skirmish with a rather slippery piece of Rocquefort when the office door flew open and the clerk erupted into the department.

'It's them! It's him!' she shouted, wild-staring eyes framed in an ashen face.

'Who's them?' asked the exasperated buyer.

'Buck House and they want 18 pounds of cheddar. Please come and speak to him,' pleaded the girl.

'How do you know it's Buck House then?' asked the buyer.

'He said he was the Prince of Wales.'

'The Prince of Wales is a pub on the other side of Brompton Road,' he explained to his crestfallen clerk.

Then there is the Floral and Fruit and Vegetable Hall. Harrods has its own nurseries at Barnes and the rest of the flowers come from the new Covent Garden market, as do the fruit and vegetables. Many of the Food Hall buyers are up before dawn making their way to the markets. The florist buyer rises at 5.15 a.m., and the meat buyer at 4.30 a.m. to start his journey to Smithfield market. The earliest riser of all is the fish buyer who clambers out of bed at 2.45 a.m. to get to Billingsgate on time.

The Meat Hall, possibly the most famous part of Harrods, has received only cosmetic changes for it is protected from fundamental alteration by a preservation order. Apart from a few new cold cabinets the only innovation in recent years came when the charcuterie department was moved into the centre of the Hall. It is a marble floored room of immense size and with a soaring ceiling; a most striking feature is the design upon the tiling walls. Entitled 'Scenes from the hunt', they are the work of W. J. Neatby and date from 1902. It is the most photographed area of the entire store.

The fresh fish display, just across the hall from the meat department, is another frequently photographed site. Every day the display is different and reflects what is available. Occasionally Harrods buys a particularly interesting fish in which case it will take pride of place in the display. In July 1979 two unusual ones made their appearance. One was a male sturgeon which was 7 feet 11 inches long and weighed 280 lbs. The texture of sturgeon is more like meat than fish and is nicest when smoked. The other fish was a 6 feet 6 inch porbeagle shark. This fish is harmless in the sea but is rather tough to eat unless marinated. The male sturgeon and the porbeagle shark were both cut up and sold for £6 and £1.25 per pound respectively. The following month a 45 lb smooth ray was on display but not for sale as it is inedible. But the largest fish of all in recent years was a sturgeon of a monstrous 11 feet 6 inches which weighed over 500 lbs. Caught in the vicinity of the Dogger Bank and brought into Lowestoft, it was the largest ever landed on the East coast of Britain up to that time, October 1977.

The queue in the bread department sometimes reaches right into the Central Hall and the perfumery department. Apart from 128 different kinds of bread, the bakery also supplies birthday cakes to order and to pretty well any design. One of the more outlandish of recent years measured 3 feet 9 inches by 2 feet 6 inches, weighed 1½ hundredweight and cost £425. The scene depicted was a finely detailed living-room in which three people were seated watching television. On a separate table stood another small cake and a digital telephone. Everything was edible. At the other end of the scale the department has received an order for a soft bread 'bap' roll costing 14 pence to be sent by special delivery which involves an extra charge, to an address in Victoria, London SW1.

Bread left over from the previous day is never sold. Rather than throw it away it is given to one of a few different charities. One of these is the St Mungo Community Trust for homeless men. The trust does a run every night of the year distributing soup and bread when they have it; also clothing. Do the recipients on their lonely vigil appreciate the irony of their food's origin?

The confectionery department has its moments as well, notably at Easter and, while the neighbouring bakery is selling 30,000 hot cross buns, it contrives to fuel the public with ten tons of Easter eggs. In 1978 a giant Easter egg was displayed that had a value of £70. It was not sold, however, as the store had decided to send it to the Hospital for Sick Children, Great Ormond Street.

But if these two departments are always busy there is one time above all when they really go mad – at Christmas. Indeed the operation that is mounted throughout the Food Halls for the Christmas trade is on the grand scale. Thoughts about a Christmas Season are first entertained up to eighteen months beforehand; this is because the store likes to offer exclusive lines of merchandise which means ordering well in advance. What looks like a fairly straight-forward gift pack may include work done by printers, basketmakers, pottery workers and packing materials experts quite apart from any food and preparation thereof.

A typical Christmas idea was the introduction in recent years of a Port and Stilton pack. Suggestions are presented to the divisional manager of the food section and he encourages, discards and coordinates until he feels he has a marketable theme. Then follows the working out of estimated sales and costs. By this time the store is in the thick of the Christmas season and there is no time for anything except the present. Then there is the sale and all the queries that follow to be dealt with and it is spring before the beleaguered buyers can turn their thoughts once more to Christmas.

Finalized ideas are presented to the managing director who decides what is to be put into the Christmas catalogue as early as April; this has a direct bearing on quantities to be ordered as items in the catalogue naturally can be expected to do better than those not included. That is what is hoped anyway!

As the summer wears on cartons and goods are assembled on the third floor of the Harrods building in Trevor Square; in August the hamper packing operation begins, gradually gaining momentum through the autumn.

In September the pigs that will become Harrods' famous York hams are slaughtered. The store is the largest retailer of York hams in the world. They are the result of a process which involves rubbing salt into the legs of pork and then having them laid down in cellars kept at a steady 36 to 40° F; the salt rubbing is then repeated several times and eventually the ham is hung to dry. It is a laborious process but natural, and has the advantage that the customer does not finish up paying for the extra poundage that pumping water into bacon can cause.

And then the Christmas season is once more upon the Food Halls, 60 tons of Christmas puddings, 2,500 birds, 10,000 mince pies, all destined for the nation's stomachs.

And thinking of Christmas brings us to the wine department. The selection of wines is extensive – wines from France range from a modest but palatable Beaujolais to Chateau La Tour at around £50 per bottle. There are wines from all over Europe as well as from South Africa, the United States and Australia. You may not find Harrods has the cheapest wine list in the world but some rare items can be found if you are looking for something different.

Harrods has its own labels for spirits as well as the normal range and some hundred brands of whisky are sold. The department is proud of its liqueurs and port section; unusual drinks like 'Inca Pisco', a concoction direct from the jungles of the Amazon, are available – for many years it was exclusive to Harrods although recently it became manufactured on a commercial basis under licence in Italy. 'Monte Alban' is worth a try if you are not squeamish, for floating in the amber tequila-like liquid is a small worm, apparently a great delicacy. It is yours for only £10.75 a bottle.

A few years ago the display department stockroom was near the wine cellar and bottling plant. One of that department's staff was a little bored one day and saw a discarded model lying in the corner waiting to be thrown away. He cut off its little finger and devoted his considerable artistic talent to making it as lifelike as possible and subsequently played practical jokes with it. On leaving the stockroom one day, again bored, he threw his creation into what looked like a stack of boxes on its way to the incinerator. Here the most dramatic part of the finger's life began. It landed in a box containing empty bottles bound for the bottling plant; and it had fallen directly into one of the bottles. The rest of the story has an inexorable inevitability about it; somehow, and nobody knows how, the bottle slipped through the normally stringent examinations in the bottling process. The first Harrods knew of the matter was a distraught telephone call from a lady who had undergone a somewhat traumatic experience at a dinner party ...

The wine cellar at any one time contains between a quarter and half a million pounds worth of drink at 1980 prices. The odd disaster has inevitably occurred, as when a member of staff made a minor mistake one evening when closing down the machinery. Over the weekend 500 gallons of sherry syphoned itself into a 100 gallon tank.

In 1977 the wine department had on display what was believed to be the largest bottle of port in the world; a bottle of Taylor's 1963 vintage port which will not be ready for drinking until 2020. Called a Nebuchadnezzar, it contained the equivalent of 48 bottles of port and would have retailed at that time at £6,000.

The health juice bar, together with the health food counter, caters for the ever-growing trade flowing from those people who thrive on ginseng, seaweed, biochemical tissue salts, concentrated garlic, apple cider vinegar and bran.

The Food Halls are where Harrods began and they are still right at the heart of the business; they account for over half the total transactions of the store although not, of course, over half the trade today. They are a different world in themselves and if Harrods had nothing else it would still be world famous.

Yashmaks and see-throughs

Next door to the Food Halls is 'Leisure Man' which is an area devoted to casual wear for men. A spiral staircase in the centre of this department leads down to 'Junior Man' which has two sections, one for boys' casual wear and the other boys' school wear. Harrods is the outfitter to several public schools throughout the country and there is an equivalent department for girls on the first floor.

Entry to the main area of the Man's Shop is effected by crossing a bridge within the store from the Leisure Man department to the men's personal tailoring section. The bridge spans the entry to the Hans Road receiving bank and was built between the wars. There is a basic ready-to-wear section as well as the personal tailoring service where suits are made to measure. Typically at any one time there are approximately 10,000 shirts and 9,000 ties ranging from a few pounds to a thousand pounds to choose from; yes, Harrods has sold ties at £1,000 each. Menswear has been one of the fastest expanding areas of the business in recent years, and in fact it is now not remarkable for the Man's Shop to outsell the fashion floor at times.

The men's hairdressing salon is just underneath the Man's Shop and a staircase near to Door 2 takes us down to a traditional barber's shop. If it is a short back and sides you are looking for, 'Get it at Harrods.' This is not to imply that you cannot have the full fancy treatment if you want it; you can and pay the full fancy price for it too.

Next door is The Green Man which is a traditional English pub in the midst of a department store. It is an excellent rendezvous for a lunchtime gin and tonic.

Walking out of the Man's Shop towards the central lifts and the perfumery department, there is a marble staircase leading down to the basement. At the foot of these stairs is a steel grid barring further progress. It is the safe deposit. You ring the bell and wait; after a few moments footsteps approach, sounding like the doorman of Dracula's castle. It is a reassuring surprise when the footsteps turn out to belong to a courteous Harrodian.

You are asked to identify yourself and if already one of the customers give your individual password, chosen when you first registered. Keys clank in the door and it swings open. The brown and cream painted decor with floral patterning looks like something out of the Victorian era; it is. The safe deposit at Harrods opened in January 1878 and has not been repainted in a hundred years. But, far from looking seedy and run down as one might expect it is preserved in beautiful condition. The whole area is one gigantic steel box, as impregnable to fire and illegal entry as human ingenuity can make it. The security systems are, of course, modern and the place bristles with sound sensors and closed circuit television cameras. There are row upon row of deposit boxes of varying sizes and you can withdraw your box and take it to a cubicle rather like a large telephone kiosk. However, it is a kiosk with the same ornate decoration, lockable from the inside for secrecy.

There are also three strong rooms where more bulky items may be left in chests or cases. These rooms may only be entered under the watchful eye of the attendant who keeps a wooden truncheon to hand should you become troublesome.

As he leaves each evening the manager sets the time clocks and checks that nobody is left inside, for once the area is secured there is no opening it again. Slowly he swings shut the three tons of steel that is the entrance door and as it closes the great steel bolts slide home and the circuit locks solid. Nothing can open that door until morning.

Also from the Man's Shop you may hear some heartbreaking whimpers, some vigorous yapping and the occasional genuine woof. It is the kennels where customers are asked to leave their dogs while shopping in the store. The tear-jerking scenes at parting and the overpowering joy at the reuniting that the attendant witnesses in the course of a day make his an emotionally demanding job.

The rest of the ground floor houses the fabrics and beautiful silks and cottons; Harrods buys materials from all over the world, including China and the Far East. Along the front of the store is a selection of fashion accessories that range from the exotic to the mundane, the stationery (Harrods still markets its own), fancy leather goods and handbags departments. The gift department, photography, the pharmacy and the silver and jewellery halls make up the rest.

The ground floor is the busiest part of the store and as a result it is unbeatable for one particular activity – people-watching. It must be one of the best places in the entire world for this sport. The cross section of nationalities and types is endless and dress varies from Bermuda shorts to flowing saris, from blue jeans to bowler hats and pin stripes, from black robes and yashmaks to see-through blouses. Accessories range from absolutely priceless rings and bracelets to safety pins for the nose and ears.

Snippets of conversation heard in isolation can prove entertaining, from the 'Darling! What a marvellous basket of fruit. Can't you think of anyone we know who is ill?' to the 'Well, they are supposed to have everything – what's so difficult about stuffed emus?'

Rags and riches

Each floor at Harrods has its own particular feel and if the ground floor is permeated with the noise and bustle of an international market place, that of the fashion floor is much more relaxed, the pace being more measured and the lay-out spacious.

Of all the merchandise for which Great Britain is famous none surpasses its knitwear, and no self-respecting tourist should ever leave without purchasing some. Harrods, of course, has its fair share of the most famous of all – cashmere. The expense and softness of cashmere wool are legendary but perhaps its most important characteristic is its ability to keep the wearer warm for so little bulkiness and weight.

The wool begins its life high in the hills and mountains of remote China. There a special breed of goat grazes and cashmere wool comes from the underbelly of this animal. It is combed out and patiently accumulated; it is so light and fine that it takes the wool from the bellies of two animals to provide sufficient for one ladies' cardigan.

There is a wool even rarer than cashmere, that obtained from the vicuna. This comes from a relative of the llama which makes its home high in the inhospitable foothills of the Andes of South America. In gathering wool from a vicuna the animal is destroyed and this has led to a serious decline in its numbers. An embargo was declared and remains in force.

Then there is the fur salon. An ice blue carpet and crystal chandelier provide a fit setting for showcases of musquash and mink, Canadian squirrel and Russian fox. There is a small room at one end where the really valuable furs are to be found; Harrods thinks the customer about to spend tens of thousands of pounds should have a certain amount of comfort in which to contemplate such a purchase. Whether or not the fur trade should exist at all is a matter of opinion but as long as it does the overriding consideration for stores such as Harrods is that they should not provide an outlet for the poacher's snare nor a market place for the skins of endangered species.

Then come evening dresses, hats, the bridal room and the breathtaking international rooms with dresses costing over £1,000. The departments merge into one another vying for the attention of the browser – in fact everything that any woman could want, ranging from the trendy cheerfulness of Younger Set to the sophisticated elegance of the Designer Room.

One of the more exciting events on the calendar of the store is the fashion show; there are two each year in the spring and in the autumn, held in the fashion theatre on the third floor. Each lasts a week and each show approximately fifty minutes. Planning starts weeks before, with buyers putting forward ideas for features. The management team of the floor, which consists of the divisional manager and three section managers, makes the final selec-

(*above left*) Henry Charles Harrod, founder of the store

(*above right*) Charles Digby Harrod, responsible for building up
Harrod's Stores and eventually for selling the business

Harrod's Stores Limited in 1892, shortly after it was turned into a
limited liability company. The photograph also shows The Buttercup
public house, later absorbed into Harrods

(*left*) Richard Burbidge, who became general manager and then managing director, and who was given a baronetcy in 1916

(*below*) Sir Woodman Burbidge, with his wife and their daughter Alva at an Avon Valley Coursing Club meet

1898 – the first escalator in England is installed at Harrods,
in what is now the perfumery department

(*above*) The Harrods bakery department *c.* 1925

(*opposite*) Harrods staff was reduced by 2,000 as a result of the First World War recruitment; instead of 'Green men' at each door women took their place

(*below*) A Harrods van in 1905

The 3-ton door which guards the entrance to Harrods Safe Deposit, 1922

e Cornish produce display, 10–15 March, 1930

Sir Richard Burbidge II, the last of the three Burbidges who were managing directors of Harrods

Harrods (Buenos Aires) in April 1931

The Meat Hall between the Wars

FIRST PRIZE

A Harrods van converted into an ambulance during the Second World War

At Harrods, Mrs Winston Churchill with Air Commandant Lady Welsh, director of WAAF during the Second World War

VE day 8 May, 1945

Harrods Toy Fair, signing the Visitor's book under the supervision of Father Christmas, 1931

The Harrods chocolate factory, 1934

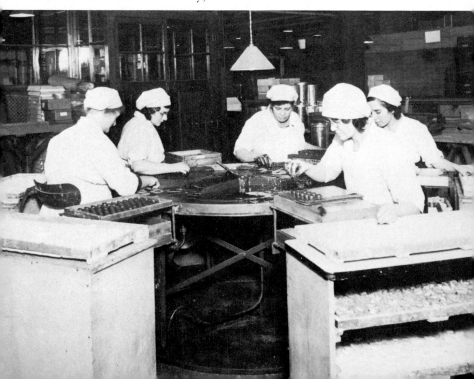

1849 ~ 1949

Harrods of 1849 ———— A Centenary Souvenir

In celebration of the Harrods Centenary, 1949

Enid Blyton signing copies of her books 20 August, 1946

Richard Dimbleby with the Coronation Robes of King George VI and the Queen Elizabeth which were exhibited at the store

Sir Hugh Fraser and his father, outside Harrods in 1959

(*opposite above*) Damage to the store after the bomb explosion in the house and garden tools department, 1976

(*opposite below*) Harrods got a midnight call ordering a baby elephant in 1975. It was for Governor (now President) Ronald Reagan of California and was dispatched by Les Wilson

Mr Robert Midgley
(in the dark suit) and
Mr Aleck Craddock in
the store

Harrods today

tion in concert with the merchandise director. Together with the show's director they have the pleasant task of auditioning the girls and choosing those who have the right faces, figures and carriage to show off the fashions of the year to their best advantage. The production itself is mounted to the highest professional standard with great care being taken to get the lighting, setting and music just right. Contrary to what one might believe, this is born of a systematic and almost obsessional attention to detail rather than a flash of creative genius on the part of the producer. Rehearsals are frequently stopped and alterations made to the sequence, the lights, the music, even the clothes. The tension rises and tempers get frayed, but come the opening the presentation is slick and professional. It is hoped the audience is thrilled by the dazzling display of quality fashions presented with flair and panache; dresses for evening wear, suits for formal occasions, separates to relax in; swimwear and holidaywear that has the men taking a sudden interest and the women resolving to diet again; beautiful furs in such profusion that £200,000 worth may be on the stage at one time.

The children's shop finishes off the first floors. It caters for Harrods' youngest customers starting from the maternity department, through the baby shop to the two to seven year old age range in the children's shop and up to the young teenager in the junior fashions department. It figured prominently in the shopping spree of £35,000 in one hour conducted by a distinguished Middle Eastern diplomat a few years ago on the occasion of his daughters starting at a new school.

The personnel department is inundated with hundreds of letters each year from young girls aspiring to be fashion buyers. Although, like most glamorous sounding jobs, it involves routine hard work, it is also a good career provided a girl has strong feet, a strong back and a resilient temperament. Once her letter has reached Harrods the young hopeful will be invited to the store for an 'open afternoon'.

The afternoon is spent learning about the store, doing

one or two tests and going on a tour of the building. Should both the girl and the store still be interested in each other after this, a second interview follows and then shortly after she will be offered a job or not. The trainee intakes are in September to dovetail with the academic year. After a week in the training department, her first job could be to act as a dresser for one of the models in the autumn fashion show. The music, the models, the clothes, the whole atmosphere can be quite overwhelming.

Her next job might be as a sales assistant. The Christmas season is getting under way and it will be a lot of hard work. Everyone who has never done it always looks upon the job as fairly undemanding but the truth is that there are few occupations that are quite as exhausting – a mixture of physical stamina and emotional resilience are called for that comes as a surprise.

After a year the girl comes before a selection panel if she wants a place on the Executive Training Scheme. It is an ordeal. Four formidable people sit behind a long table and one of them may be an actual fashion buyer. The trainee has to introduce herself and say a little bit about her life to date. Next she has to take part in a group discussion with the seven other people applying with her. It involves answering a letter of complaint from a customer who is aggrieved at having been called a 'bloody foreigner' by a member of the sales staff. It is a real letter although the department has been changed. Then she has to do a maths test. The first responsibility of a fashion buyer is to be able to subtract the cost price of a dress from the selling price and end up with a healthy figure, so maths 'O' level is far more relevant than art 'A' level. A personal interview with one of the members of the panel follows. And then finally comes the part of the interview she has been dreading most, the practical test. The only thing she knows for certain is that there will be two helpers to whom she must be nice. All eight applicants sit and wait like victims in the dentist's surgery, hoping it will be over quickly. The training officer is saying something to her: 'Miss Wilkins, we have a task for you to do; how you go about it is entirely up to you. You have the facilities of the training department at your disposal and two members of staff over there to help you. For the purpose of this exercise the panel does not exist. Here is your task ... Please begin now.'

Our trainee is given a piece of paper on which it says:

'This bag should contain two cotton reels of each colour. Your task is to make a list of the missing reels you would need to make the pairs complete. You have five minutes.'

The trembling girl looks in the bag she has been given and panic grips her. It is full of cotton reels and they are all blue; dark blue, light blue, mid blue, royal blue, turquoise blue, sky blue, navy blue, and a whole range of colours she has never heard of – aquatone, saxe blue, gobelin, majolica ...

Somehow she will manage to get through the job with the cooperation of her two helpers and is judged on her performance accordingly. Either she is offered a place or advised that her application has not been successful, in which case she is asked to make an appointment with the chairman of the panel to discuss her future. She can have another go at getting a place in February.

The Executive Training Scheme course lasts nearly a year and a half, at the end of which the girl should be ready for the job of supervisor.

A year passes and she becomes an assistant buyer. Two or three more years pass and she begins to wonder. But then at last one day a member of her staff comes to her and says, 'The managing director's office on the phone for you.' She discards a customer who is on the point of spending £2,500 as if she were a typhoid carrier and rushes to the phone.

'Can you come up and see the managing director at 3.30?'

And at 3.45 she is a buyer. She can hardly believe it; a real life, genuine Harrods fashion buyer.

She might go to the *Prêt à Porter* in Paris, the mecca of fashion. It involves making contact with the local Associated Merchandise Corporation office in Paris which acts as an agency and an advisory service to buyers who are outside their home country. American in origin, it operates all over the world and is particularly active in Europe. The AMC has prepared an itinerary which will help the buyer to make the best use of her time.

The collection is laid out like the Ideal Homes Exhibition but on three floors and with 3,500 exhibitors. It is important for the new buyer to work systematically otherwise she will become confused and finish up buying anything just to get through in time. So our buyer walks the entire three floors before narrowing down her interest to the few suppliers with whom she will do business. The merchandise she has bought will arrive in the store in six months' time. Shortly thereafter she may go to America or to a fashion centre in Europe, like Milan. Finding the right merchandise is always something of a challenge, especially to the new buyer, but she can go into the shops or stores that sell her sort of merchandise and look at all the labels on that merchandise. Then she can check the manufacturers' addresses in the phone book and visit those she likes. This together with the advice given by her merchandise representative from the AMC will see her through.

The merchandise she buys could be featured in one of the fashion shows, if not in the main one then, perhaps, in one held just for her department. There are a few of these each year, notably in the Calypso room where the models and swimwear on view can be guaranteed to improve the rate of male customer flow on the fashion floor.

Any fashion show involves a great deal of fast changing behind the scenes and by the end the girls reach the stage where they can be forgiven for not knowing just what they are wearing ... or not wearing. Recently a model glided off the stage in her bikini, whisked it off and slipped into a wraparound skirt and halter top and was out on the stage again leaving the horrified dresser staring helplessly at a pair of pants that should not have been in the dressing room. The model danced down the stage in time to the music and, reaching the end right in front of the audience, brought the show to its finale with a flamboyant twirl ...

A house is not a home

Ranging from the bare necessities of life to pure frivolities, the second floor has something to interest almost everyone. It is devoted to household goods of every kind.

There is the luggage department; prominent amongst the display is luggage made in Harrods' own leather goods factory and just to walk through this department precipitates a strong attack of wanderlust. The desire to fly off somewhere just so as to have a reason to buy the beautiful luggage that smells of real leather is almost overwhelming. The floorboards there creak because the level of the floor is at variance with the surrounding areas as this elevation is the oldest part of the Knightsbridge building still standing and when additions and alterations were made it was not possible to reconcile all the different levels.

Passing carpets from the Orient, Persian rugs of exquisite design and craftsmanship, there are the pianos from the most famous makers in the world like Bosendorfer, the piano that the great Oscar Peterson chooses to play; and then there are the concert grands from the likes of Steinway and Bechstein, the magnificent Grotrien Steinwegs and in recent years some very fine specimens bearing such names as Yamaha and Kawai. Next door is the world of hi-fi, music centres, record players, cassette recorders, radios and televisions. The cacophony of several sets playing simultaneously has something of the sound and excitement of a great orchestra tuning up before a concert – or it may be enough to drive you out of the store! At least the situation is not as bad as it used to be; some years ago the room was shared by the record department and the strains of Beethoven and Beatles music could also be heard vying with each other. However, even that was but a passing whisper compared to the noise coming from the neighbouring pet shop which used to pride itself on its large and extremely vociferous collection of parrots.

It is hard to believe that a haven of peace is close by – the book department, with one of the largest selections of books in the world; whether your particular preference is for history or politics, music or the arts, thrillers or romances, paperbacks or children's books, Harrods' book department will cater for it. To add to the tranquillity it is one of the most effectively air conditioned areas of the entire store and on a baking summer day that fact alone makes it worth a visit. Should you have a question that nobody can answer then look for a bearded gentleman in his shirt sleeves; he is always there and he always knows the answer. If he doesn't it simply means you have got the question wrong.

And then we are into the china and glass departments; like British knitwear, British pottery is second to none. Each year the china buyer sets off for the 'Potteries' around Stoke-on-Trent to find out what is new and different and to place the orders for the coming year.

Stuart and Waterford are names that feature largely in the glass and crystal rooms next door. And you can use the service for beer tankards and other glass to be personalized. On Friday, 4 May 1979 Britain's first woman Prime Minister took office. An engraved goblet was ordered from the glass department which was wrapped magnificently in the gift wrapping department and delivered to the new Prime Minister's home. It read:

Margaret Thatcher
Prime Minister

4.5.79

The most notable thing was the confidence of the customer to place the order ten days before the general election.

Just like the china buyer, the glass buyer makes an annual pilgrimage to the source of his merchandise. A visit to the Waterford Glass Factory might be typical. In the morning he would be driven from his hotel to the factory and at reception introduced to the lady who is to be his hostess for the day. Her usual duties are to take groups of tourists around the works but a major glass buyer such as the one from Harrods rates a hostess to himself.

She shows him first the show room where there is a display of glass that is powerful testimony to the skill of the craftsmen of the factory. Pride of place in the display goes to a cabinet in which are some of the original pieces made by the firm in the mid nineteenth century; Waterford is older than Harrods and as proud of its history.

Next he sees the sand and silica mix that will go into the kilns to be heated to searing temperatures before it is worked by the master in one of the four 'chairs' who blows it into the required shape, be it a glass, decanter, bowl or one of the many other shapes. A gatherer then gathers the molten glass and carries it to the liar; this is a belt that takes it through a gradual cooling process to prevent splintering, cracking and spontaneous self-destruction by over-rapid cooling. The masters in the chairs work on piece rates and each time they complete a piece they chalk it on to a blackboard which the supervisor consults at the end of the day to calculate wages due.

At the end of its spell on the liar the glass is removed to trays by girls who reckon to lose about 5% to 8% of the blank glass, which is glass without markings, due to faults and breakage. They send it to another belt on which it has any surplus top knocked off before it is ready to go to the cutting room. Here more girls sit in rows wielding a machine that looks like a suspended spirograph; this puts felt lines on the blank glass for the cutters to follow. Then he sees the artistry of the cutters with their carborundum wheels each specializing in a certain type of cut, some vertical, some horizontal and others flat cuts. The speed and dexterity of the cutters is astonishing, particularly when the value of the glass they work on is considered.

When the cutters have finished their work the glass goes to the grinding shop and from there to the polishing shop where it is dipped in a bath of acid to give it that showroom sparkle. The final part of the operation consists of inspection and packing after which it is taken to a container ship in the Waterford harbour.

The glass bound for Harrods will go from Waterford to a warehouse in Bedford. Once a week the Waterford representative checks the Harrods stock and brings it up to the agreed basic levels. The orders placed on Monday come into the store on a Thursday and such is the relationship between the two companies that if Harrods says that a piece of Waterford crystal is unobtainable you will not find it elsewhere unless of course it is a piece that another retailer may have left in stock.

The glass buyer also visits Italy each year. The trip starts in Milan with the 'Macef', a trade fair of china, glass and gifts. From there to Venice, and the 'vaporetto' to Murano, where he spends the day working along the main canal. Here are many small family run businesses which will make pieces to order; this allows the china buyer and the glass buyer to coordinate their purchasing and to make those special buys that stand as showpieces in a Central Hall display from time to time. As the glass buyer talks you can gain something of the excitement and satisfaction that he finds in a job that allows him to travel to out of the way places, climbing up creaking staircases into dusty attics to find works of true craftsmen for display.

A pin to an elephant

Popular folklore has it that Harrods will supply you with anything at all from a pin to an elephant. If you want an elephant the place to go is the pet shop on the second floor. It would not be in stock but it is not many years since the store obtained a rhinoceros for a buyer, so maybe you would be lucky. There is of course the well known story of the hoaxer who telephoned the store and facetiously said he wished to buy an elephant. Whatever the reply he had expected he certainly was floored by the one he got:

'Yes, sir, an Indian elephant or an African one?'

In fact, the pet shop no longer stocks the crowd pullers that once it did and even its name has changed from 'The Zoo'. The introduction of quarantine laws for exotic species placed severe restrictions on a trade such as lion cubs for a start, and there are many obvious problems in caring for wild animals in a department store. Take, for example, the occasion when the store received an order for a pair of exotic snakes. Memories vary as to the species but it seems likely they were Indian Rock Pythons; they do not vary upon what transpired when the two snakes reached the building.

They arrived, a male and a female, in a professionally prepared and humane packing box, where they were kept for two days whilst awaiting despatch to their new owner. Well, there is, of course, not a lot to do in a cardboard box and if you were locked in a bedroom for two days with an attractive member of the opposite sex what would you do to pass the time?

The moment arrived for their new owner to collect them and he brought with him his own box which he preferred to take them away in. The swop was duly made and the empty box despatched to the 'burnhole' to be incinerated. It appears there was rather a backlog of work down there and the box was left for several weeks in the warm atmosphere and by the time it was finally destroyed four baby snakes had glided silently away into the Harrods woodwork, so to speak.

No further thought was given to the event until some months later a young female assistant from the china department was carrying an exquisite Royal Doulton dinner service across the china warehouse in the basement not far from the burnhole. Suddenly she deposited the priceless china in a heap of smashed fragments on the floor. Her story, amid screams, that she had seen a snake was treated with the sort of impatience one customarily hands out to people who try to invent ridiculous excuses for acts of carelessness. Subsequently four allegedly different snakes were seen and two were caught. There are those that point to a reduction in the rodent population in the basement ever since that time and draw the conclusion that four minus two is two ...

But back to lion cubs. It is the exception that is as fortunate as a certain young cub called Christian; he was bought from Harrods and raised in an antique dealer's shop in the King's Road, Chelsea. However, the inevitable problems of space, food, exercise and safety soon began to bring problems. Crisis point had been reached when into the shop walked actor Bill Travers of *Born Free* and *Ring of Bright Water* fame. An introduction to Christian was effected and he was returned to the plains of the Serengeti, where he belonged. The full story of this project is told in the book *A Lion Called Christian*. But many of the lions reared in captivity are sold to zoos, few of which provide satisfactory conditions for such a magnificent animal; most are probably just destroyed because their owners have tired of the heavy responsibility of ownership or the novelty has worn off.

Today, the pet shop concentrates on dogs and cats. The choice ranges across many of the popular breeds and Harrods pedigrees are impeccable. Of course there is a penalty to be paid on the price tag, but all the care and attention lavished upon them is fully in keeping with their aristocratic connections.

When puppies or kittens arrive they are taken to a kennels/cattery where they are given two days or so to recover from the stress and fatigue of being removed from their mothers and travelling to London. One of the animal tenders makes sure that they settle into their new surroundings; this means combing and grooming and in cases where particularly close supervision is required they will even take them home with them. Some breeds settle much more easily than others; labradors and old English sheepdogs are especially placid but alsatians do not relish the zoo-like environment at all. You will, in fact, usually be disappointed if you look for an alsatian; this has nothing to do with the breed's reputation for unreliability, which is any case far more often a reflection on the owner than the dog, but simply because it does not settle well.

All animals have their temperatures taken every day and a record is kept so that any sickness can be detected early. The recommended immunization injections are given and the cages cleaned out every day.

The pet shop is one place where Harrods will invoke its right not to sell unless it is satisfied that adequate and humane facilities exist for the future care of the young animal. There were no qualms on that score for one lucky young pup recently. In 1979 Roscoe Tanner reached the finals at Wimbledon and only just failed to topple the King of Wimbledon, Bjorn Borg. He had just become the proud owner of a Harrods Yorkshire Terrier, 'Wimbledon 79', known to his friends as 'Wim' and as puppy owners will testify acquisition of a puppy is at least equal to fatherhood in demands and worries, but the new responsibilities took their toll on the centre court. Roscoe did his best; he flew Wim to the USA on Concorde so as to minimize inconvenience to the little fellow. He came back in 1980 to show the pet shop buyer the photographs of the 'dog party' thrown for Wim in America.

Harrods has recently banned dogs in the store even if carried; there are kennel facilities provided near to Door 3. When this rule was first brought in the staff were instructed to stop offenders and direct them to the kennels. The management also posted a 'No Dogs' sign on all the entrance doors. Owing to a proliferation of other signs on the doors concerning credit cards accepted the dog signs were approximately eighteen inches above the ground – 'Dog eye level,' explained a spokesman. On one occasion in the linen department the then sales manager who is certainly one of nature's gentlemen discreetly spoke to a rather formidable lady about the matter:

'Give me a chance,' she boomed, 'I've only just bought the bloody thing.' The linen department is two rooms away from the pet shop.

Ancient and modern

Of all the selling floors the third is the one on which it is easiest to become lost; it is a seemingly never ending jungle of furniture and the way it is laid out in a series of small self-contained rooms, while attempting to enhance the attractiveness of the displays, does nothing at all for the sense of direction.

A newcomer to the store could be excused for thinking that furniture is all that there is on the third floor. However, there is also a bathroom shop crammed with circular baths, conventional shaped ones in every imaginable colour, and bathroom accessories in profusion. It is a department that smells good as well.

Also on the third floor is the department children dream about – the toys. The first room you enter is full of cuddly objects: owls, otters, Paddington bears, frogs, dogs, hippopotami, Muppets of all shapes and sizes and of course the traditional teddy bears. Harrods devotes almost as much space to cuddly toy animals as to real live ones. The next room is an Aladdin's cave of the latest childrens' diversions. From the proven favourites such as train sets to the latest computer-based technological wonder, the choice is mind-boggling. A busy department at all times, the Christmas season sees it grow into an operation of truly formidable dimensions, spreading itself into the adjoining fashion theatre.

Plans for the Christmas Toy Fair have to be laid months in advance and the merchandise is ordered by the buyer almost a full year ahead. A small army of sales staff, packers, query clerks and supervisors needs to be assembled and trained for the three-month onslaught. Not least of the difficulties is making special arrangements with Father Christmas to ensure that he will be available again; it has always been Harrods policy to have the real Father Christmas as opposed to the imposters found in some other stores.

The danger of making do with a sub standard Father Christmas can be illustrated by something that did not happen at Harrods but, in fact, somewhere else. A lady and her little girl went shopping one December day in 1979 and duly went to pay a visit to Santa Claus. He had a very charming chat with the little girl, to whom he gave a small present, and they went on their way with their spirits uplifted. Sitting on the bus on the way home the little girl, who was very pleased with the present she had received, turned to her mother and asked:

'Mummy, what did Father Christmas give to you?'

'Oh nothing to me darling; he only gives presents to children.'

'No, Mummy, he gave you a present; I saw him put it into your bag.'

A grim realization of the truth that was dawning on the woman was confirmed when the bus conductor arrived at that moment to collect the fares; her spirit was not the only thing that had been uplifted – her purse had gone. When she finally managed to get home she telephoned the store to inform them what had happened; she made it clear that she was making no wild accusations on the strength of what her daughter had said but wondered if they could investigate the matter. The security officer of the store found the lady's purse in Santa's locker ... and some others; better stick to the real Father Christmas at Harrods.

Near toys is the largest private lending library in the country. Rumours that it is about to close have circulated for as long as anyone can remember but it is still open. The argument for closing it revolves around something business studies experts call prime contribution per square foot; the argument for keeping it open is illustrated by the story of an expert running a department store. He scanned sales figures and quickly noticed that fashion goods had the highest profitability margin. He got rid of all his other merchandise and soon he had four floors of fashion goods. Further arithmetic showed he was making his highest profit on evening wear and he devoted all four floors entirely to evening wear. One particular dress had the highest profitability of all; he got rid of all the rest and proudly presented to the world a store of four floors all selling the same garment. After the liquidation he went back to business studies school.

Harrods has always been managed with a mixture of head and heart; let us hope there will always be a place for anachronisms such as the library.

The main business of the third floor is nevertheless the furniture. The range runs from the genuine antique to contemporary space age designs; from the famous names in furniture like Ercol to the lesser known specialists at the very top end of the market. If you buy something from the furniture floor and the salesman is worth his salt he will try to sell you something else to go with it; it is called a 'second sale' and is a standard part of any good salesman's armoury. However, not even the most optimistic could have foreseen the course of events when, a few years ago, a young woman and child wandered through the furniture area one lunchtime. At length an antique dining table took the lady's fancy and she spent some time discussing it with the salesman. In the end it came to light that although the table was irresistible to her it would not fit into her house as it was a modern house with modern furniture.

'Ah, well, I can't really solve that one for you, madam,' replied the salesman.

'Well, maybe you could ...' she said. 'Hasn't Harrods got an estate office?'

'You can't really mean that you'd sell your house just so you could have the table?' responded the incredulous salesman.

'Oh, good gracious, no,' came the reply, 'I was thinking of

buying a second house; you know, a sweet little cottagey type thing and the table could go in it.'

The new world

Until the 1970s the fourth floor was devoted in the main to offices and workrooms; now it is a thriving selling floor. The change was initiated in the mid sixties when Way In was opened as Harrods' answer to Carnaby Street and the high-street boutique; it includes a restaurant and a hairdresser, and the range of merchandise is extensive for both sexes. How long the visitor spends there depends on their tolerance to pop music; if it is high there is a great deal to see; if it is low escape quickly into the newer, neighbouring Way In Living. This aims to be Harrods answer to Habitat.

Next door is a fascinating old maps and prints department. The Desmond Groves Portrait Studio is nearby and you do not have to be rich and famous to have your photograph taken there.

Travel at Harrods operates from the fourth floor. There is a Thomas Cook's as well as the Export Bureau which also incorporates the London Tourist Board. A great deal of Harrods business is done on an export basis as the store is very much a tourist attraction and welcomes millions of visitors from overseas each year. Its image as a London base for oil sheiks is considerably exaggerated, however, and the bulk of trade is still done with the home customer, whom the store has been at pains to woo in recent years. Then the greatest volume of sales is done with visitors from Europe, followed by America, and only then the Middle East.

Opposite the export desk is the Credit and Service Bureau or the 'Where do I go to complain?' department. It is more than that. The Service Bureau deals with a never ending succession of callers with queries that range from the mundane to the bizarre. Typical are those on account charges, credit sale agreements, complaints about rudeness by staff, customers demanding to see the managing director, customers wishing to express appreciation for good service. The safest rule of thumb to operate is 'if in doubt, ask at the Service Bureau'. Even if it turns out to be the wrong place they will at least be able to direct you to the right one.

Opposite is the Harrods Trust, offering a complete banking service and having the advantage of being open throughout store trading hours. Its service includes a Bureau de Change where foreign money may be exchanged.

Opened in 1976, Olympic Way covers the area formerly occupied by the boardroom and directors offices. Built with an eye to the increased interest in sports and keep fit, it offers a comprehensive range of sports clothing and equipment.

Nearby is the chief cashier's office. He is responsible for all the cash handling arrangements in the store and an awesome responsibility it is. In these days of plastic cards it is still hard cash that is the most frequently used method of payment and twenty-five per cent of Harrods' business is paid for in cash. The largest sale made by the store and paid for in cash to date is one of £82,000. The customer did not actually produce 82,000 pound notes; instead the store had to collect the money from a bank. The largest sum actually produced by a customer in the store in settlement for a purchase is £36,000 in the jewellery department.

The amount of cash taken in a day naturally varies according to the time of year but it is always substantial and a section of the chief cashier's office called 'Checkline' has to collect it from the department cash registers throughout the day, sorting it, allocating it for the records and banking it. Another part of the operation sorts and packages coins; called the 'Coin Centre', it has five machines processing £6,000 per day between them. It also provides the floats for the 300 registers in the store.

The new plastic money, credit cards, accounts for fourteen per cent of Harrods business but this particular sector is growing. Cheques account for twenty-one per cent of the payments. This does not include cheques used to settle monthly accounts, which account for twenty-three per cent, virtually all accounts are settled by cheque. Naturally Harrods suffers its share of bouncing cheques; in that respect it is not unique but perhaps one or two of the situations that arise as a result are, as in the case of the cheque paid for a lion delivered to a customer. The cheque bounced and when Harrods recontacted the customer the reply was to the effect that the animal was in a cage with three other lions and that if the store wished to repossess the merchandise it was welcome to try!

The women's hairdressing and beauty salon is on the fourth floor and offers full beauty treatment. At the back is a children's hairdressing salon with a delightful animal design on the wallpaper. During the two sales in January and July this area is used as a 'lost children's department'. There are always some youngsters who get separated from their parents and if they are found wandering around the store by the staff they are taken up to this collection point. Needless to say the operation is not without its traumatic aspects and there are usually more hysterical adults than lost children to be found.

Just along the passage is the picture gallery. This department frequently has displays of leading contemporary artists as well as doing a brisk trade in reproduction prints. Prices range from tens to tens of thousands of pounds and there is also a framing and restoration service.

And so to the Harrods restaurant just beyond. At either end is a bar serving pre-lunch cocktails – at the picture gallery end it is the ordinary lounge type but at the other is the new Trafalgar Bar with its uncompromisingly nautical decor, and a magnificent painting of the Battle of Trafalgar dominating the room. In the restaurant room itself, there is usually a pianist providing an unobtrusive musical accompaniment to the meal and on occasion some strolling players serenade diners; at Christmas, carol singers add a touch of seasonal goodwill to the proceedings.

The restaurant features a traditional English menu, with roast beef and Yorkshire pudding always a strong attraction. The steak should be good, being prime Aberdeen Angus from Harrods' own meat department. The cold table always looks delicious and the sweet trolley presents almost irresistible temptation to cast diet and caution to the winds.

Behind the scenes an army of chefs and waitresses keep things running smoothly; or as smoothly as things ever run in restaurants which as a genre seem even more susceptible to disaster than shops. The kitchen is ruled by the head Chef who prowls among the steaming cauldrons making sure that everything is being conducted to Harrodian standards.

There are, of course, a number of self-service buffets dotted throughout the store. The first of the present generation was the Dress Circle which opened on the first floor in 1968. It was followed by the Upper Circle on the fourth floor, then by the Way In Circle and most recently by the Leisure Circle on the Ground floor.

Shortly after the Leisure Circle opened, one of the cashiers was distracted from his work by the sound of raised voices. Looking up he saw two women arguing about who was first in the queue. One decided to settle the matter and strode purposefully to the cash register; the other, a German lady overcome with frustration, took the only remaining course open to her – and threw a particularly juicy egg mayonnaise at her retreating combatant. Just as the cashier was about to take some vicarious amusement from the incident fate intervened. The first lady reached the cash point and placing her tray beside it leaned over to reach for some cutlery. The movement took her out of the line of the flying plate; the cashier took a full portion of egg mayonnaise right between the eyes.

On the first day of the sale a few years ago the Harrods restaurant was packed and a gentleman wishing to be helpful went to the cash desk with his Harrods account card to pay. The machine that imprints the card details on to a bill was standing on a table; in the rush it had become pushed near to the edge. The assistant vigorously pressed the handle and with a crash it toppled. Directly beneath it was a fire extinguisher with its release valve dead in the path of the falling imprinter. A jet of water spurted straight across the restaurant wreaking havoc in its path. Basil Fawlty at his most inspired could not have bettered the next five minutes.

CHAPTER FOUR

Behind the scenes

Until 1980, the Estate Office used to be situated at the far western end of the store on the fifth floor at the top of the marble staircase that led up from the ground floor entrance at number 1 Hans Road. It was moved to make way for the new set of escalators which are to be built in the early 1980s, and now conducts its thriving business from a new site on the fifth floor.

During a January sale a few years ago the battle was raging fiercely and one of the directors, feeling it was time to take a look, left his office on the fourth floor and started off down this staircase. There he came upon a sight that even he, in a twenty-five-year career with the store had not seen before. There in the midst of the turmoil were four Arab gentlemen on the landing of the marble staircase down on their knees and facing east on their prayer mats.

Also on the fifth floor is the Sales Ledger/Credit Office/Sanction Office complex, the nerve centre of Harrods customer accounts. There are approximately 150,000 customer accounts and they generate around 2,500,000 transactions each year. Over the years a good many ribald comments, most of them good humoured, have been passed at the expense of Harrods' accounting system. Such quotes as 'It is not necessary to enter Harrods to be honoured with one of their bills,' have been heard since Lily Langtry's day; some were justified, some of them not, as is the way with most shafts of abuse. However, in the cutthroat world of credit today, Harrods has been forced to join the twentieth century; computers and microfilm rule OK.

The telephone exchange is nearby. Here up to a dozen telephonists sit at a huge crescent shaped board; a jungle of leads, sockets and wires faces them and a never ending series of winking lights tells them that the world is calling Harrods. The store receives upwards of 10,000 calls every day and has 140 incoming lines. Anybody who has ever tried to ring Harrods will tell you that it is not enough, but with people resorting to the telephone more and more, Harrods, in common with many other switchboards, is hard pressed to cope.

The rest of the fifth floor is taken up with an assortment of back-up services. The staff restaurant occupies a large area at the back of the building and there are workrooms and stockrooms, even a piano factory, dotted around. There is an insurance office as well as the customer services area and the personnel and training division.

Department stores in general and Harrods in particular are sometimes accused of being expensive. Harrods does not seek to present itself as a cut price bazaar but on the other hand it worries a great deal about value. How can a department store provide value for money?

The answer, in one guise or another, boils down to service and that is not to say that Harrods staff are more friendly and helpful than those in other shops. Service means more than the expression on the face of the person who serves you; it means that when you are in Harrods and have just bought a dress you can also buy the bar of soap you need on the way out. Of course you may decide that you are not prepared to pay the extra three pence that Harrods happens to be charging as compared with your local supermarket. In that case you must get into your car and drive round to the supermarket and pay to park your car and go in and buy the bar of soap for three pence less. If you were to add mileage, parking, stress and your time to that bar of soap you might conclude that it cost you more than it would have done to pay three extra pence while you were in Harrods in the first place; especially when you consider that you could have had the bar of soap delivered to your home! In relation to its competitors Harrods' range and services are still the yardstick by which any department store in the country must judge itself if it aspires to usurp the throne.

There are three main components of the Customer Service section and we have already seen the credit and service bureau where personal callers go.

The second part is the Clerical Services area, where all incoming mail arrives. Harrods receives approximately 18,000 letters each week rising to 32,000 at Christmas and all are delivered to the post room where they are opened and immediately divided into two groups – those containing some form of payment and those not. The former are placed on a moving belt and disappear to be paid into the bank by three o'clock on the same day. The latter go on a moving belt in a different direction which takes them to the reading room. Here they are sorted and redirected throughout the store or dealt with if they are queries.

A query is channelled into one of four categories – home queries, 'QTS', management queries or export queries.

'QTS' stands for Query Transfer Service which is applied to all queries where there is only one department involved and the nature of the query implies a relatively easily remedied human error. So if you ordered a green one and the store sent you a red one and you wrote in to query it your letter would become a QTS. The relevant department must answer the query and return the letter to the Customer Service department within twenty-four hours.

Home queries are given to a clerk whose job is to follow the query through the system, resolve it and communicate with the customer. It usually involves two or more departments or is rather serious in nature.

A management query is one where the customer has addressed the letter to a director either by name or title and is dealt with in much the same way but arrangements are made for the director to whom the query was addressed to be kept informed of progress and often to write the reply.

The Export Office backs up the export bureau and also contains the Shipping Office, which handles the despatch and documentation of all goods being exported by sea or air freight. Just imagine the scope of queries when merchandise is being sent to Texas, Tehran, or Timbuctoo.

Queries are a rich source of Harrods 'stories' but as they usually involve considerable inconvenience to customers the store is not given to seeing the funny side of them! However, sometimes they go on for so long and become so horrendous that a bond develops between the query clerk and the customer. A case in point was the occasion of a lady giving Harrods a substantial order to replan and refurnish her flat.

All the details were duly agreed and the lady went to Canada for six weeks, the estimated time for the job to be completed. She returned filled with excitement and anticipation at seeing her transformed home. Not one brick had been moved, not one carpet laid; nothing had happened at all. Her disappointment and several more powerful emotions were quickly registered with the store and there followed two weeks of such feverish activity as has not been seen in England since the repeal of the corn laws. The lady went away for a further short period, the miracle was wrought, and Harrods met the deadline. On the day before her return the service manager decided to satisfy himself that everything would be to the customer's liking upon her return. The inspection confirmed that it was and he stood on the new carpet in the new lounge looking at the new ceiling and heaved a sigh of relief that registered on the anemometer on the meteorological office roof. As he cast his eyes heavenwards, however, he saw something which appalled him. Water was dripping through the ceiling; the flat above had a burst pipe and within hours had wrecked the lady's new home ...

By the time the job was finally complete the service manager and the lady had cemented a relationship which should be able to withstand anything.

Then there was the occasion when the carpet layers went to an estate of identical new houses and did a first class job of carpet laying in number six. It turned out to be of relatively small comfort to the customer when he moved into number four.

Working in customer services for any length of time leads to the firm conviction that Harrods never does anything right, but the reality is, of course, different. The store deals with approximately 30,000 queries each year which sounds astronomical until it is put into perspective by comparing it to the 15,000,000 transactions carried out annually. Perhaps it sounds better to say that out of 15,000,000 transactions each year 14,970,000 go right as far as the store knows.

The customer services section also deals with mail orders and telephone orders amounting to £2,000,000 of business in a year. There is a typing pool which produces 1,500 letters each day and 2,500 at Christmas, and in total the store sends out 15,000 letters per day rising to 25,000 at Christmas. There is also a telex service; a message tube service for in-store mail; a central filing service; a gift box section at Christmas ...

A typical conversation could be the service manager on the telephone to the company secretary.

'Do you know if any of the managers who come to work by car live anywhere near Sevenoaks and would be prepared to do a delivery tonight on their way home?'

Something else has gone wrong but with a little bit of luck the customer will never know. She may think it strange that her merchandise is delivered by an executive-looking person in an executive-looking car at nine o'clock at night ... but then Harrods always was different.

No account of Harrods would be complete without mention of the letters it receives; they range from eulogy to abuse. Inevitably some demand, 'What is Harrods coming to these days?' but it is not true that people only ever write to complain; some grateful and satisfied customers write and some contrive to remain pleasant and cheerful even when they have every right to complain bitterly, as did this gentleman:

Dear Sir,

About ten years ago my wife and I passed the Carlton Hotel in Cannes in a ramshackle old Volkswagen and we promised ourselves that we would spend a holiday there when we had made our fortunes. Unfortunately these are still pending being made and the likelihood of me treating us to a holiday at the Carlton is still very unlikely. In desperation my wife therefore decided to treat me to a two day 'quickie' break complete with sea view (£29 per day extra). As a result of this magnanimous gesture I thought the very least I could do to emulate her generous move was to purchase a pair of swimming trunks on our account from your store and this was duly done.

I am not sure whether it was the metabolic upheaval to my system at the thought of the £75 per night (b & b) prices or the nightmare of £10 per day to lie on the beach, but disaster befell my beautiful swimming trunks – a hole burst in the crutch! Fortunately this was no major disaster for two reasons a) the following day it rained like hell all day and b) there were so many nude women on the beach that everyone seemed too preoccupied to notice the hairier parts of my body.

We were surprised at the quality of the stitching because it had not even been strained as I purposely bought size 36 when I am only a 34. However, on our return my wife subsequently sewed up the offending aperture and that, I hoped, would be the end of the matter. Unfortunately it wasn't; we have subsequently taken a short break at the Imperial Hotel, Hythe and upon my initial launch into their indoor swimming pool a further disaster happened. My beautiful swimming trunks split asunder! Luckily one of the housemaids lent us a needle and cotton and the gaping hole was duly bodged. You can imagine my surprise and dismay when two days later the pocket fell off having never had more than air in it.

We are now only $4\frac{1}{2}$ weeks away from going on our annual pilgrimage to the sun – a giant extravaganza with the whole family to Ibiza – and I am therefore wondering whether you could see your way clear to letting me have, say, a fiver towards the cost of a new pair of trunks which I will probably get from – dare I say it? M & S.

Please don't think I will hold this incident against your store. I am a very happy and satisfied customer and will continue to enjoy shopping at Harrods, but quite seriously at £14 odd for a pair of trunks they ought to last more than a day or two, shouldn't they?

Yours faithfully,

P.S. I enclose the offending remains.

The customer was sent two pairs of swimming trunks with the compliments of the store! As he has not been heard of again it is presumed that either they proved satisfactory or that a similar incident occurred and that he is now languishing in a continental gaol for indecent exposure.

Everyone likes praise and Harrods is always pleased when some comes its way; fortunately this is not unknown as the following letter from a lady in Woking demonstrates:

Dear Sir,

For many years I have purchased at your store and if you will forgive me I would like to tell you a few things that I am sure you must already be aware of.

Firstly, you are infallible, and I really mean that! Every time I telephone or call your employees are so helpful and courteous and their knowledge of everything is quite unbelievable. Do you know I can quite understand why Her Majesty The Queen shops at your store; to be served by Ladies and Gentlemen is such a pleasure apart from the fact you sell quality. I really would recommend you all over the world but then I know there is no need to – you are world renowned.

I haven't given you my address because I do not want to give you the trouble of replying but I just had to put pen to paper and tell you what wonderful employees you have and what good judges you must be. There's no store like Harrods!

Yours sincerely,

Then there are the letters from those who have found something at Harrods quite out of the normal run of things and have written to say how much joy this has brought into their life:

Dear Sir,

On 16 November 1977 my husband gave me a treat I had always wanted; a trip to the pet department at Harrods, (it was our honeymoon). I had been breeding cavaliers for several years, but dearly wanted a rare papillon (butterfly dog). Imagine my surprise when he said 'There are two papillon puppies in the corner' (I had been trying to get one for years!). Imagine my delight when he bought one (whom I named Nicky – 'Nicongetti of Rumbavant') on Access!! Well, since then, Nicky has become an outstandingly good specimen of his breed; he has won dozens of prizes and has sired three lovely litters; recently he has been tipped as champion quality so we shall take him to big championships next year.

Every November since 1977 we come to your pet department and on Thursday next 29 November we shall be there again, but we have not seen any more papillons and do not expect we will as they are really rare. We just want to say a very big THANK YOU.

Yours sincerely,

How pleased they were when they found that the store did have another papillon – a female whom they bought as a companion to Nicky.

Back down to earth when something like this lands on the service manager's desk:

Dear Sir,
I feel that I must write to you and express my deep regret at the lack of service now available at Harrods.

On the past two Saturdays, I have been shopping in various departments in the store and have, along with other customers, been subjected to various degrees of rudeness and indifference from members of staff ... unfortunately it would appear that Harrods staff have been instructed that it is more important to serve foreigners first rather than Londoners who are very regular customers ...

or:

Dear Sir,
A few days ago whilst on a brief visit to London I had the long awaited pleasure of visiting Harrods.

It was indeed a pleasure to visit the various departments and to admire the vast array of goods and services provided. However, I have one criticism which I feel I must bring to your attention. I very much regret that on several occasions I found it necessary to seek the advice and help of certain members of your staff and that they responded in quite rude and off-handed ways.

Despite the fact that your staff appeared busy, I still found it a surprise that in a store, renowned throughout the world for its service to its customers, certain members of the staff seemed to lack basic manners and common courtesy ...

The letters quoted are taken all the more seriously for being couched in objective reasonable language. Appropriate action is taken and replies sent.

Then there are letters from the store's younger customers:

Dear Sir
Last week when our school visited Harrods I bought some cakes and perfume but I was very annoyed when I saw that my friend had bought a record cleaner in a green cover with Harrods printed on the front for 40p and a fantastic postcard for only 5p. I was fuming when I realized the wonderful items I had missed so I am begging you to please please send me the record cleaner and the postcard bought with my fifty pence postal order if you wont send me these two items please could you send me my postal order back as I am only twelve years old and rather short of cash at the moment.

Yours very hopefully

PS If you do send me the postcard and record cleaner I will open an account at your wonderful store when I am older and have married Prince Charles.

Sometimes a little detective work is required to clarify requests as customers do not always ask for exactly what they want; like the lady who wanted a copy of the book *Rum, Bum and Concertina* by George Melley:

Dear Sir,
... Please will you send me a copy of *Gin, Sin and Mouth-organ* ...

Then there are the letters from staff which are downright amusing – like the Irishman (yes, really!) who wrote to complain of dismissal:

Dear Sir,
I am writing on behalf of meself ...

Or the two girl students who were contemplating a medical career and thought they should find out whether they had strong enough stomachs:

Dear Sir,
We are writing to enquire if you have any temporary summer jobs working with corpses in your funerals department ...

Sometimes the sequence of events outlined in letters of complaint is so bizarre as to tax credulity. Some, of course, are fabrications and others totally unfounded but a story that survives concerning a letter received in the late 1960s is typical of the things that have happened over the years. A lady ordered some finest lamb's liver from the meat department to be delivered by Harrods van. The vanman duly arrived at the house but was unable to get any reply to the doorbell and so he decided to use his initiative. Although he found nobody he did find a half open kitchen window at the back of the house, expertly lobbed the package through the opening and went on his way, cheerful in the knowledge that another problem had been successfully dealt with.

However, all was not so well in the kitchen he had left behind. Here it was wash day and the washing machine was of a venerable age, only performing to the accompaniment of much clanking and shuddering. The lady thought she heard the doorbell ... no, it can't have been ... putting it out of her mind she opened the top loader and took out the first wash of the day and put in the second. All the while she was quietly worrying in case the doorbell really had sounded. She decided to check and leaving the top of the machine open went to the front door. There was nobody there although she did notice a Harrods van parked just two doors down the street. Closing the door she returned to the kitchen and without a further look slammed the top of the machine shut and started the cycle ...

The moral of this tale is that before starting your washing machine you should always check to see that a pound of lamb's liver has not been inadvertently thrown into it by a passing Harrods vanman!

In case the reader should be left with the impression that rudeness and inefficiency are inevitable these days here's an incident that occurred not in the nineteenth century nor even the 1930s, but in the 1980s.

A lady arrived in London from Los Angeles. Suffering from jet lag and exhaustion she decided to do her shopping by telephone and rang Harrods to order four bicycle bells at £2 each. The telephone call was made at 4.00 p.m. and the lady, convinced that the assistant had got the details wrong, rang off feeling sure that was the last she would hear of the matter. Imagine her pleasant surprise when the bells were delivered to her at 5.00 p.m. with a letter expressing the compliments of Harrods. She wrote back to the store:

Dear Sir,
... a perfect ending to a lousy day ...

CHAPTER FIVE

Working in a different world

A few of Harrods' Landmarks as Trade Pioneers:

H ONESTY.

A SSIDUITY.

R ELIABILITY.

R EPUTATION.

O RIGINALITY.

D ISTINCTION.

S UCCESS.

Pioneers of free delivery to Country.

Pioneers of Shopping by Telephone.

Pioneers of all-night Telephone Service.

Pioneers of Special Shopping Trains from the Country.

Pioneers of extra week's holiday for all Territorials in their employ.

Harrods equipped the C.I.V.

Harrods supplied the largest Carpet in the world (Olympia).

Harrods equipped the " Discovery " (Antarctic Expedition).

Harrods supplied the first Xmas Hampers for Cripples (over 3,000).

Harrods have been honoured by visits from H.M. The Queen and Royal Family, as well as by almost every Royal Personage in Europe, and many Indian and Eastern Potentates.

One of the facts about Harrods that most seems to impress the casual observer is the number of staff who work in the store, usually quoted as 5,000 rising to 6,000 at Christmas and during the two sales. However, like most things in a large organization the true picture is somewhat more complicated.

To begin with there is more than one way of calculating staff numbers. For accounting purposes Harrods deals in 'full time equivalents'. An FTE is a person who works more than 30 hours per week. Someone who works over 20 hours but under 30 hours is deemed to be half an FTE and someone who works less than 20 hours a quarter of an FTE.

The lowest level that staff numbers fall to is in the spring of the year and at this time there could be as few as 3,500 FTEs. The highest number comes in the week of the January sale with perhaps 5,000 FTEs.

The actual headcount is complicated by the fact that not everybody who works for Harrods is employed by the store. There are many people who are employed by outside companies, such as in the perfumery department where the major houses provide their own staff to man their counters. So when all is taken into account the lowest 'headcount' would be 4,500 and the highest over 8,000.

The recruitment, training and management of a workforce of this size is a major operation and to cope with it is the job of the personnel and training division.

Recruitment at Harrods never lets up. Approximately 15,000 applicants for jobs are dealt with each year and of these approximately 5,000 are engaged. Similarly about 5,000 leave the store each year. Although that sounds like one hundred per cent turnover of staff it is a little misleading. The pattern is that about 3,000 are permanent, and the other 2,000 turns over two and a half times during the year staying for only six to eight weeks during the summer or at Christmas time or indeed for just two weeks at the January and July sales.

The recruitment team consists of five people who are responsible for the entire operation. To begin with they must establish the vacancies. That may sound easy but when you are dealing with a workforce of 5,000, even if ninety per cent of the positions are filled, you still have 500 vacancies. Keeping track of them is not as easy as might be supposed, particularly when the situation changes daily with some being filled and others falling vacant. Having established the vacancies, some thought has to be given as to where likely applicants are to be found and appropriate advertisements placed. Some jobs are naturally easier to fill than others but the store is in general by no means immune to the problems of recruitment that all the major employers in the central London area face.

Once a person starts work at Harrods the recruitment team bows out and the new recruit becomes the responsibility of the training department. Here he is introduced to the intricacies of Harrods selling systems. These are naturally somewhat extensive as the more services that a store offers the more systems it must have to cope. Indeed there is an internal publication entitled *Systems Manual* which runs to 256 pages.

Quite apart from the induction of new staff the training department runs a number of schemes for school leavers and those wishing to pursue careers in the store. The main ones are:

The retail trainee scheme This is a programme of training for school leavers between the ages of sixteen and eighteen with no particular academic qualifications but an abundance of enthusiasm, common sense and a desire to succeed. The trainees are placed in a number of job assignments during their first year, where they are encouraged to learn at first hand the business of retailing. They also attend college outside the store to study for a nationally recognized diploma. If they pass the first year they continue to the second year which is conducted on much the same lines as the first but at a more advanced level.

The career trainee scheme This scheme is for school leavers between the ages of eighteen and twenty who have passed two 'A' levels and 5 'O' levels. The course is conducted in the same way as the retail trainee programme but it is of one year's duration only. It is a more intensive course and the college work is at a more advanced academic level.

The executive trainee scheme This is the programme of training within the store that prepares 'high fliers' for a position as a supervisor. It is by no means easy to get on to this scheme as the standards Harrods sets for its future management are very high and competition is fierce. Candidates are selected from university graduates, successful retail and career trainees and from internal applicants from the store. At any one time Harrods may have between eighty and one hundred executive trainees and at the successful completion of the course they are promoted to the position of first line supervisor within either the selling or non-selling areas of the store.

Training does not end with the executive training programme and out of store courses are run by the central training department at the Harrodian Club premises at Mill Lodge, Barnes. The House of Fraser has a residential training college at Burnham in Berkshire and Harrods staff take part in the courses that are run there. In recent years the House of Fraser has taken over Wadham College, Oxford for a week each autumn and 120 people from throughout the company have attended a week's training, again with Harrods staff participating.

However, policy was not always so enlightened and the present personnel manager delights in producing a copy of the employment contract in use at Harrods in 1891. A facsimile is shown opposite.

Things have moved on a little since those times and today's contract runs to 10 pages, spelling out the rights of the employee in unequivocal terms. The process of change really got under way in the 1920s when the managing director of the day sent for the personnel manager and told him to form a staff council, thus beginning the practice of joint consultation between management and staff, which continues to this day.

Union membership at Harrods dates from the 1930s when it began with some of the small craft unions – the hairdressers, the tailoring garment workers, the cabinet makers and so on. The main shop workers union USDAW was not formed until after the Second World War and only slowly gained strength at Harrods. By 1970 it had become sufficiently established for the company to recognize it officially and to enter into a recognition and procedure

IMPORTANT

NOTICE.

You are requested to observe

that all Employes are engaged

subject to Dismissal Without

Notice.

HARROD'S STORES, *Limited.*

February 18th, 1891.

agreement. Agreements were also reached with the TGWU and the AUEW and today Harrods recognizes ten trade unions.

All the staff representative bodies meet with management once a month in the Store Council to discuss things both sides regard as important and the opportunity is thus provided for the staff to have a voice in the running of the store as far as those things that affect them are concerned.

A further part of the central personnel division is the staff clinic where a doctor and three full-time nurses are employed to provide an on-the-spot medical service for staff, and indeed for customers also. Most things medical have happened on the premises of Harrods and although it is not certain whether this includes birth it certainly includes various types of sudden illness and death.

The personnel function is a vital part of the life of the store and has existed for over seventy years. There are records of employees going back to the last century in its 'dug out' or store cupboard where all personnel records no longer actively required are kept. Well over half a million people have joined and left Harrods since it began and a great many of them are still faithfully recorded.

Imagine a small town with a resident population of five thousand; those five thousand people serve a world-famous tourist attraction and play host to 25,000 or 30,000 people every day; they naturally have their share of law and order problems, especially when one considers that on the first day of the two sales there is the equivalent of a Wembley Cup Final crowd. The local constabulary (Chelsea Police Station) is, of course, not permitted to patrol the store in the normal course of events as it is private property.

Harrods has a security team which numbers around one hundred and provides twenty-four-hour-a-day cover. The nerve centre of this operation is in the basement and from here the chief security officer and his men have combated in the last few years armed robbers, extortionists, shop-lifters, pick-pockets, handbag thieves, cash register thieves, forgers, confidence tricksters, arsonists, terrorists, hooligans and the out and out nutters. He also controls the fire station and a squad of fire prevention officers. The fire station is on the second floor of the main building and from there it is possible to monitor the progress of any emergency. Fire doors seal off one section from another

throughout the store and precautions are exhaustive, including heat sensors in every room. Their job is to sense
higher than usual temperatures or smoke density and they
are backed up by a system of sprinklers activated the
moment any danger threatens.

Harrods has suffered few emergencies over the years and
the majority of jobs undertaken by the chief security
officer's team are quite mundane in character; they include
the opening and closing of the store each day; in itself
this is no paltry operation – it takes at least an hour to open
the store and the same to close it.

It is a sad fact the net of the security department
catches a number of staff members. Naturally Harrods is
open to the professional crook who obtains employment
but they are few and far between. The vast majority of
staff offenders are first time amateurs and it is perhaps the
most tragic thing in the life of the store when a young
person has to be prosecuted for petty thieving.

The main job is the everyday shoplifting and pilferage
that all large stores suffer from these days. Practised professionals can lift up to a whole rail of dresses at a time
and equally professional techniques are required to combat
them, naturally they remain trade secrets. Almost any type
of merchandise is vulnerable. Many professionals operate
in gangs with one member of the gang distracting the
attention of the sales assistant while others do the lifting.
A particularly dangerous moment is closing time when
staff have one eye on getting away and their concentration
is elsewhere. There have been several cash bag snatches
at this time of day although surprisingly few seem to succeed. The milling crowds at Harrods exits should provide
good camouflage for the escaping thief but in practice serve
only to slow him up. Many of the people around Harrods
at that time are members of staff and security men have
been able to use their help to detain cash bag snatchers.

The complexity of store geography seems to work in
Harrods favour in frustrating escaping crooks. However
good their reconnaissance may have been they often become

flustered in the heat of the chase and take a wrong turning
and are cornered in a cul-de-sac. A gentleman who snatched
some money out of a cash register in the book department
a few years ago started on a high speed tour of the second
floor which took in china, glass, luggage, house and garden
tools, kitchenwares, hospitality, major household, electrical, pianos, radio and television, back into books, through
to carpets and into the pet shop; there he turned into the
area where the exotic animals were kept and was caught
under the interested gaze of two lion cubs.

The more dramatic incidents of recent years include
two much publicized robberies. The first was a wages
snatch in the basement involving firearms and culminating
in one of the gang being found shot dead in the taxi that
was used as a getaway vehicle. The second was the theft
of a cash collection bag and the thief was reported as
making his escape over the roof. The picture of a chase
across the rooftops of Knightsbridge and escape down a
rope thrown over the parapet of the store to the Brompton
Road five storeys below, leapt into the imagination of those
reading the account in their Sunday papers.

What actually happened was that the hold up took place
on the roof. Cash registers have to be emptied during a
trading day and their contents banked. Many different
routes are used on cash collection runs and it so happened
that on this day the roof was used. If you climb the stairs
from the ladies hairdressing department to the fifth floor
you will find two swing doors which provide access to the
roof; a very short walk across the roof (about twenty yards)
brings you to a further pair of swing doors which lead down
a ramp back on to the fifth floor. Here the hold up took
place and the assailant escaped back into the store and
eventually out through the front door. He was subsequently
caught, since when precautions surrounding the movement
of cash in the store have been tightened, with the roof no
longer being used.

Extortionists have a record of unmitigated failure with
the store; don't they know the parent company is Scottish?

Its first consideration, however, has to be the safety of its customers and staff as when, in the mid seventies, a telephone call came threatening an explosion unless a £500,000 ransom was paid. Terms were agreed; a taxi would collect the money from a Harrods Green man. The taxi arrived and a Scotland Yard detective dressed as a Green man climbed in with an attaché case full of London telephone directories. When the switch took place in Lowndes Square the man never knew what hit him.

Likewise a failure was the 'gentleman' who walked into the store with a device looking exactly like a bomb, demanding to see the managing director. After a brief discussion with a security officer built like a Welsh second row forward, the man took fright and decided to run for it; such was his hurry that he dispensed with the normal formality of opening a plate glass swing door and ran straight through it landing in the arms of two policemen who just happened to be passing!

The security team and all the management carry a sophisticated battery of radio transmitters and 'bleeps'. Three male members of management were riding up in the lift with one female member. Out of the blue and apropos of nothing the lady remarked, 'Mine always gets sensitive in the lift.' That she was referring to her bleep was not the first thing that came into the minds of the startled three!

When a customer is confronted by a rude sales assistant his/her immediate feelings are indignation and embarrassment. Depending on how aggressive the customer is the next stage is either to start complaining loudly or to leave the store as quickly as possible. Either way the likelihood of a sale being completed is very low. Harrods has moved some way towards offering the customer a greater degree of self-selection but of all the major retail outlets it remains the one most committed to personal service. It is tempting to see the problem of rudeness as one of declining standards whereas in reality it is very much more complex than that.

Obviously there have been changes in the social relationship between customer and staff over the past 100 years and we have moved towards a somewhat less class conscious society. This means sales assistants are less willing to take rudeness from customers – a fact some customers find hard to accept.

Secondly there is an inbuilt conflict of demands in the sales assistant's job. A high level of social skills – a good appearance, clear and fluent speech, literacy, numeracy and communication skills, diplomacy – are required. But personal ambition in terms of career progress, social status and financial reward has to be low. The two demands are often incompatible, as is obvious.

The conflict inherent in the demands leads to the third part of the problem which is the high number of sales assistants who do not regard the job as a career and they may just be filling in time. The climate of employment is another factor that plays its part. Job security for the employee has become immeasurably stronger in recent decades, he is much more inclined to assert himself and his position and sales assistants are no different to any other group of people in this respect. Finally in any transaction there is, of course, the chemistry between assistant and customer.

So what can Harrods do about this? Terms and conditions of employment are obviously most important. Good wages and conditions do not of themselves cause sales assistants to work hard and be polite but they do obviate some worries. In general pay at Harrods stands up well to comparison with other stores but the management has it under constant review.

However, the fact remains that the most important single factor in influencing attitudes is education and training. Discipline may influence behaviour but it will often entrench negative attitudes even more strongly. What do Harrods teach their sales assistants to do and say? Since Charles Digby Harrod started to build the business saying cash and courtesy counted, the store has tried to maintain a high standard of service and manners. It has not always succeeded as well as it would like and as the 1970s wore on management felt the issue had to be tackled afresh. A number of events brought matters to a head; a stream of complaining letters from customers whose grievance seemed only too justified; the knowledge of the management that sales figures could be considerably improved by offering better service; and a trip to the United States by the managing director where standards of salesmanship are in a different league all combined to produce action.

There was a storewide campaign to get everyone to smile more in 1977. Many businesses have tried this from time to time and results are usually mixed. For every member of staff who enters into the spirit of the thing and smiles more there is another who gets 'bloody-minded' and refuses to smile at all. However, Harrods went ahead undaunted and the campaign was launched at a party for the buyers and managers given by the managing director on a Thames riverboat. After an evening of drinking and dancing on the vessel they were all smiling nicely. The next morning, by which time some of them were not smiling at all, a series of champagne breakfasts were held in the store for the four hundred supervisors. To give the staff something to smile about one hundred winter weekends in Majorca were on offer for those whose colleagues voted them the most friendly and helpful people in Harrods.

Did it work? Nobody can really prove it one way or the other. The winter weekends were won so somebody must have been smiling and at least the letters of complaint from the customers abated somewhat.

The following year Harrods put the accent on professional salesmanship. By this time the Jubilee tourist boom was a forgotten dream and trade was not nearly as buoyant, so there were no boat trips or weekends in Majorca on offer. A bonus scheme for staff was introduced and a campaign launched entitled 'Go for the Bonus' in which staff were encouraged to divide customers into three groups, red, amber and green, like traffic lights. A red customer was one who had no intention of buying anything and was in the store for any number of reasons apart from making a purchase. An amber one was the browser who if approached with the time honoured 'Can I help you?' will answer 'No, thank you, I'm just looking.' The green one knew what to buy and approached the cash till with her purchase in one hand and money to pay for it in the other.

Treatment by staff was modified accordingly. The green customer should be served without delay; the amber customer should be left to browse but not to flounder. The assistant should acknowledge the customer's presence with a pleasantry or two but not crowd her too much. The art of the sales assistant is to ensure amber customers turn green and the bulk of the programme was devoted to suggesting ways that this could be achieved. The red customer should be acknowledged but not pestered. If she enjoys being in the shop she may be tomorrow's amber and next week's green customer.

Did it work? Like the smile campaign it is hard to judge but the subject is regarded as so important that in recent years the House of Fraser has employed someone full time to write selling training programmes for every conceivable line of merchandise to be used countrywide throughout the entire group. No expense has been spared even to the extent of providing all the stores with video recording equipment to allow salesmen to see themselves in action.

Imagine the dullness of a routine job on a routine day lifted when Paul Newman is suddenly standing in front of you. Staff learn some interesting things about the characters of the famous who shop in the store; in the case of Paul Newman his eyes *are* every bit as brilliant a blue and his manner every bit as charming as his screen image. Naturally serving celebrities is not always a pleasant experience; some of them can be arrogant and ungracious but fortunately these are few and far between. Harrods has always attracted the famous and there are still those that can remember Lily Langtry as a regular customer. The privacy of its customers is paramount and the staff should offer efficient but discreet service to the well known. But there can be recognition problems sometimes. Whilst comparatively minor actors are instantly recognized, leading politicians and industrialists from abroad may be unknown to the staff and, given the predeliction of some of the world's richest men for dressing like walking advertisements for Oxfam, embarrassing moments are inevitable.

No such problems occur with sports personalities, who are quickly recognized. Wimbledon fortnight always produces its fair share of tennis stars in the store and Arthur Ashe, Roscoe Tanner and Dennis Ralston come to mind as recent visitors who were true ambassadors for their sport. So too were Mark Spitz, David Wilkie, David Broome and Nick Faldo for theirs.

Musicians come, and one memorable visit was that of Oscar Peterson who, after autographing records in that department was persuaded to sit down and play at the Bosendorfer grand piano in the department next door. Whether one enjoys jazz piano playing or not it is impossible not to be impressed when in the presence of genius and it was clear that, in his own field, he was, and is, just that.

Book signings bring in celebrities, both in terms of famous novelists, as well as people who have become famous from their lifetime achievements and written their stories, such as Dame Margot Fonteyn whose visit stands out as particularly good. A successful book signing session is an occasion to remember; so too is a session which flops. There are few things more embarrassing in store life than having an eminent person sitting in the book department with nobody asking him to sign his book! Harrods has been known on a few such occasions to resort to rounding up staff from other floors and having them take a copy of the book for signing; so if you are offered a book which is signed by the author and inscribed 'To Geoff, with best wishes,' you will know what happened.

Of all the famous people who have come to Harrods in recent years, however, there can only be one number one. A sales assistant in the book department was dealing with a typical pre-Christmas morning's trade. She had just made a sale of some books to a customer who had paid by cheque, and as it is a store rule that cheques must be approved by a senior in the department, she looked around for her assistant buyer. He was nowhere to be found. Cursing the fact she set off round the department and, after a fruitless five minutes was getting desperate. The queue at her till was mounting by the minute and everyone was getting thoroughly impatient. She made for the buyers' office somewhat irately. Reaching the doorway her path was politely but immovably barred by a very pleasant but extremely determined gentleman. She looked past his shoulder into the office and the strongly worded protest she was about to deliver died stillborn. It took several seconds for her to turn and walk slowly back to her counter. 'Where have you been?' asked the narked customer. To this day she does not know how she stopped herself replying, 'To see the Queen.'

'Enter a different world' may sound a somewhat pretentious slogan. Harrods is in fact several different worlds and that of the engineering division is fascinating. Climb up two further flights of stairs from the hair and beauty salon floor and you are into territory quite unfamiliar even to the overwhelming majority of the staff. Right at the top is a small notice indicating the engineering department. It is the roof of Harrods and the impression is exactly like walking on the deck of a mighty ocean-going liner, with the profusion of iron ladders, tanks, air conditioning units, fans and cabins all heightening the similarity to a ship. There is the steady hum of machinery coming from the fans. There is absolutely no doubt which of the two would have the greater impact if closed down for an hour – the beauty salon's closure for an hour would cause disrupted customers whereas closure of the engineers' department would cause the total shut down of the store.

One can watch the traffic of the Brompton Road snarling far below like Dinky Toys and look across to familiar London landmarks – The Houses Of Parliament, Big Ben and St Paul's Cathedral. Away on the horizon are the Crystal Palace television masts ten miles to the south, on top of the hill once covered by the Great North Wood; hence its present name of Norwood. And then to the west are the domes and towers of the Brompton Oratory and the museums beyond like threatening icebergs.

To enter the chief engineer's office is to enter the bridge of the ship; charts and dials are everywhere and it is no surprise to find that two of his key men learned their trade on board ocean liners. The first stop on a tour would take you to a room full of whirring situated close by, where the electric motors that power the passenger lifts of the store are maintained. The room is a microcosm of Harrods in the way that the old and the new stand side by side.

On one side of the room are the motors which power the operator controlled lifts which date from 1929; on the other side are those which power the automatic lifts installed in 1979 and controlled by a computer which stands in the middle of the room, displaying a bewildering series of panels covered in columns of winking red lights.

Moving on across the roof there is the carpenter's shop where, as well as a certain amount of maintenance work being done, they make display stands for the store, often in perspex. A little further on, right at the edge of the roof overlooking Hans Crescent, is a quaint pavilion, the familiar terracotta stonework topped with jade green roof tiling. This is the plumber's shop and at the north east corner of the roof is another similar pavilion, considerably larger, which is the painter's shop.

All over the roof are dotted air conditioning units of various sizes and dating from different periods; the very latest technology is juxtaposed with venerable plant that has been there most of the century. And then there is the dome at the centre of Harrods front elevation. There are many theories advanced concerning its purpose, with probably the most frequent being that it stands over Harrods own artesian well; the truth is that it does house one or two tanks but it is an architectural feature pure and simple.

Near the pharmacy department is a staircase leading to the basement and to a ramp that disappears into a tunnel leading under the Brompton Road to Trevor Square. Skips, like large boxes on wheels, line the route and are the main vehicles used by the store to transport merchandise within the building. As the convoy trundles laboriously out of sight an electric trolley appears and with much ringing of bells careers past and on into the tunnel.

Emerging from the tunnel you come into the despatch 'ring', a large circular table that revolves slowly under a shute. This shute is at the end of a system of conveyor belts which carries merchandise from every corner of the store and deposits it here for the despatch department to sort and deliver.

Nearby is a lift; it has an interior of wood planking and is like being in a crate. It crawls upwards and groans to a standstill and the doors open into a goods receiving yard. There are Harrods vans everywhere and the platform that runs round the edge of the yard is usually cluttered with crates and parcels.

There is another engine room with a huge metal cylinder outside which is the silencer for the three mighty engines pounding inside the engine room. The noise is deafening, nonetheless ... Every piece of machinery is spotless, in testimony to the loving care and meticulous British craftsmanship lavished upon it. Next door to the engine room is the workshop where, during the 1930s, sixty Harrods vans were built. Today, they are busy building frames for trolleys; there is a fleet of 2,000 vehicles trundling around inside the store. Next door is the workshop upon whose lathes all the axles are made.

Early one autumn morning in 1978, there was an accident in the Trevor Square engine room that led to a serious fire. A great deal of the electrical power for the store is generated from this room and soon large areas of it were being plunged into darkness. Very few customers were aware of any deviation from normal service and the Harrods tradition for coping in an emergency was upheld.

Back near the pharmacy department is another essential engine room – an insignificant enough looking room with some rather flimsy looking machinery in it emitting plaintive buzzing noises; this is where the refrigeration for many of the cold rooms and cabinets in the store is generated.

Further along the passage, which is called Kent Passage, is a hole in the wall with a staircase leading down to the main engine room, where there are rows and rows of mighty engines roaring in a cacophony of sound that is so overpowering that the visitor wriggles in discomfort.

The story of the power station in Harrods is a fascinating one and is told by the power station engineer, taken from a paper he presented to the 'Diesel Engineers and Users Association' on 26 October 1978. For the technically minded all the details are included.

The requirements of the four and a half acres site are equivalent to a small town and all water, steam, air, heating and electrical requirements originate from a central power station.

Historical review

Records show that there has been a power station in the store since 1890 when the building was gas lit and 'power' was steam harnessed to pump water, drive compressors and produce hydraulic power for lifts. The store remained independent of outside electrical supplies until 1921 – the generating plant comprising Lancashire boilers and six Willana steam engines aggregating 960 kw installed in 1908. The electrical consumption was 1,100,000 units in 1909 and this rose steadily to 2,460,000 in 1920 due in part to increased trade but also because the remaining prime movers were displaced by electric motors. Condensing was not practical and water consumption increased to 70 million gallons a year necessitating the sinking of additional boreholes. As diesels replaced steam this fell to 30 million gallons which is still the current usage.

The 1920s were years of growth and ambitious expansion of the store. The power plant had to follow suit and it was decided to include a diesel generating station beneath the new workshops being built at Trevor Square. Between 1921 and 1928 six Mirrlees, Bickerton & Day 6 cylinder, 250 rev/min diesel generators totalling 1,200 kw were commissioned. Each engine had a waste heat boiler feeding water. The diesels were an immediate success and the use of steam generating plant discontinued except during the winter heating period.

In 1934 two more Mirrlees diesels were installed in the Main Engine Room. These were 8 cylinder, 800 rev/min engines driving 272 kw dc generators. A similar engine of 300 kw was added in 1939 and this diesel remained in service until the dc system was shut down in 1977. The war halted the growth of the business and the 9,219,000 units consumed in 1936 remained a record for nearly 20 years.

After the war, conversion to ac was commenced. Site generation at 3.3 kv, grid import at 6.6 kv and distribution at 415 v was selected. None of the diesel plant was convertible so six English Electric 8 cylinder, 600 rev/min diesel alternators each rated at 300 kw were installed in place of the dc engines at Trevor Square between 1950 and 1952. The old waste heat boilers were superseded by jacketed exhaust manifold recovery. A cooling tower system was installed so that electrical output could be maintained irrespective of hot water demand.

In 1957 the two older Mirrlees engines in the main engine room were replaced by three more English Electric diesel engines driving 340 kw alternators. Though similar in designation to those previously installed at Trevor Square very few parts are interchangeable.

It took twenty years to fully load the system established during the 1950s and this also proved to be the economic life of the diesel engines.

The present diesel capacity is 3,870 kw:
3 × 650 kw Allen 6 BCS12DX installed 1977–8
3 × 300 kw English Electric 8 RK Mk I installed 1950–2
3 × 340 kw English Electric 8 RK Mk II installed 1957

The future

The last twenty-five years has seen steady growth whilst the immediate future indicates a rapid increase in electrical demand. Next year an air cooling plant is being installed which will provide cooling for a tenth of the building. This unit will have an electrical loading of 400 kw and should the scheme be extended to the whole store an extra load of 3 mw will be created. A new escalator hall and more selling areas will also boost the load.

Fortunately most of the load will be non-essential and preferential tripping will be installed to safeguard essential supplies. The initial extension of capacity will comprise three dual-fuel diesel engines of similar output to the new 650 kw engines. They will be at Trevor Square and will replace the existing English Electric sets in that station. It is intended to fit waste heat boilers producing low pressure steam for auxiliary services.

As the projects develop further diesels of higher output will be installed in the main engine room. The variety of plant in the building necessitates constant manning and a new control centre is to be built. New plant also enables automation to be installed and the remote operation of Trevor Square engines is under active consideration.

Addition to paper by the author

Since the original draft paper operations have been seriously affected by an engine room fire at Trevor Square. Fuel escaping from a ruptured bus rail ignited and the station had to be abandoned. There was little structural damage, but the remaining three English Electric diesels and associated switchgear were damaged beyond repair, one 650 kw alternater required rewinding and all wiring destroyed. Strenuous efforts limited the closure to five weeks and by February 1979, output will be back to pre-fire levels. Three dual-fuel diesels, new switchgear and extensive modifications have been put in hand for completion late in 1979. During this period of difficulty the three Mark II English Electric diesels ran impeccably with 100% availability and absolutely no maintenance.

But there are plenty of other things besides engines in the main engine room. For a start this is where the store's heat is generated. The great pounding engines produce tremendous heat but instead of allowing this to evaporate as is the case with the motor car engine, the heat is captured and used to heat all the hot water in Harrods. Even so, there is just too much for the needs of the store, which uses approximately 100,000 gallons of water per day, 40,000 gallons of which are hot, and some energy is wasted.

The central heating system of the store is fired by six great oil-fired boilers. Like gigantic kettles they are kept at boiling point to produce steam which is fed through several whirling turbines from whence it emerges at low pressure. The process is completed by a 1908 vacuum pump which looks as if it was invented by Heath Robinson himself. It is an amazing sight and one leaves it wondering how many of the machines installed today will be in spotless condition and still giving punishing and invaluable service in seventy years time, say 2050.

Three insignificant looking pipes turn out to be the source of Harrods water supply, thirty million gallons every year and every drop drawn from the store's own wells 250 feet below the building. It is sometimes stated that Harrods has its own artesian wells but this is not true, for the water does not rise to the surface of its own volition. Under Harrods flows a tributary of the river Thames; the store stands over a seam of chalk and a basin of gravel in which the underground reservoir of water collects. The volume is immense; during the great drought of 1976 the water level in the three Harrods wells did not drop at all and it is estimated that a drought would have to last for several years before that would start to happen. The only drawback is that the water although beautifully pure is very hard indeed; to compensate for this all the hot water used in the store is artificially softened. Next time you wash your hands in the store notice how soft the water is; you need very little soap and there is a smooth almost slimy feel to it. However, also notice next time you drink a glass of water in one of the restaurants how clear and sharp the taste is.

The special promotions that the store launches are some of the most dramatic events in Harrods' calendar. As well as providing a break from daily routine and adding an extra dimension to catch the imagination and enthusiasm of everyone in the store, their main purpose is, of course, to increase trade by attracting more people to the building and providing a theme for customers to see running through many of the different areas of the store.

The idea for a promotion is born in one of the directors' minds, either by a personal experience such as a visit abroad, or by the enthusiasm of one of the buyers or managers about something they have seen somewhere in the world on their travels.

'Harrods Hoists the Flag' was a successful promotion recently which grew out of a desire that Harrods, the leading name in department stores and the magnet for millions of overseas visitors, should do something to draw attention to the vast amount of quality merchandise designed, created and marketed by British firms and individuals. The idea that it is chic to buy foreign has permeated through a whole range of products in past decades, an obvious example of which is motor cars, but the same trend can be seen in fashion goods and housewares to the point where a brisk trade is being done in such things as imported ceramics and glass – areas where Britain is acknowledged worldwide to have no peers. A fact about Harrods that is not always realized is that the great majority of the merchandise that it sells is British.

Once the promotion idea is born it is thrashed out at board level to try and ensure that it is a commercial proposition and that the merchandise can be found to sustain it. The 'Harrods Hoists the Flag' promotion meant contact and cooperation from and with government agencies, the British Export Council, the British Tourist Board, airlines, hotels, the Council of Industrial Design, British Rail, the National Trust, the media ...

The display manager has to discuss window and department displays, relating it to the title of the promotion. The press officer is called in to advise on possible newspaper coverage. How about asking leading fashion editors to select merchandise of their own choice for their own window? Perhaps the same idea could be extended to the display of furniture rooms on the third floor? Divisional managers discuss merchandise that could be used. British apples, Aberdeen Angus beef, British lamb, British 'real ale', British knitwear, British china, furniture, linens and sports goods to name just a few went into the 'Harrods Hoists the Flag' promotion. Famous British personalities from the world of sport in the Olympic Way and authors doing book signing sessions ... the possibilities are endless and gradually the potential of the ideal is realized or rejected.

Whether a promotion is a success in the last analysis depends on the merchandise and the reaction of the buying public. A notable recent success was a promotion entitled *'Bonjourno Italia'* for which Harrods flew Italian chefs over to provide an authentic Italian cuisine during the promotion. Eminent Italian musicians came and gave a recital of chamber music in the fashion theatre to a dinner jacketed audience one evening after the store had closed.

The nightmare of every buyer is to be 'lumbered' with merchandise bought in specially for a promotion that flops. The buyer may well not have even bought it in the first place and will be extremely willing to think of thirty reasons why it should never have been bought and why there is no chance of selling it at anything less than a crippling loss!

Many retail concerns are now buying centrally; that is to say that a buying office purchases in bulk and distributes the merchandise to several shops who all try to sell it. Much of the House of Fraser has this system together with many of the large multiples – Marks and Spencer is an obvious example. It has self evident advantages in terms of cost effectiveness and control but one of the problems is that those selling it do not have the same degree of involvement as if they had bought it. Ask any department manager who works under a central buying system why his merchandise is not selling and he will tell you that it is because the buying office has misjudged conditions in his locality.

Harrods' stock is not centrally bought; each department has its own buyer and it does have the consequence of making the staff rather protective about their stock. Criticize the merchandise to a sales assistant and she will often become defensive to the point of shirtiness; but not when it has been wished on the department from outside – then it is fair game!

So next time you see a fine example of Eskimo art in the January sale cast your mind back a few months and perhaps you will recall that Harrods had a promotion offering the largest collection of Eskimo art outside the Arctic Circle ... but that's show business and show business is very much Harrods business and the flops of yesterday are soon buried and forgotten in the excitement of tomorrow and anyway, one of the directors has had a good idea for the next show.

The way the store is laid out, its decor, its style and its displays, are what makes it a different world and what makes it worth coming thousands of miles to see.

The story starts in the windows. There can be no finer advertisement for any store than the world famous sweep of fashion displays along the Brompton Road. To look at them is to see what Harrods is all about. Harrods needs its display team as it has approximately eighty windows and not many of them are deeper than seven feet, or as the display manager says, 'It's like dressing out a corridor.' People rarely realize the windows are so small and the team is singularly reticent about the tricks employed to deceive. However the floor and the backdrop are always covered in the same material so the eye has difficulty in distinguishing where one ends and the other begins.

The fact that Harrods' display manager is responsible not only for the windows but also for internal displays helps to prevent the problem of the windows falsely representing goods displayed within the store. If you see something in the window and only that one will do, can you have it? In some shops the answer is 'no' but in Harrods it is 'yes'. The windows are changed every week in any case and the likelihood of the departments running out of the merchandise on display in them is remote.

The coordination of a theme for Christmas or a major promotion requires plans to be laid months ahead and there are studios and workshops to cope with such projects. A theme for Christmas is agreed in early spring – say that the season's colour will be magenta and the theme of clowns will be used.

The display manager goes away to the drawing board and emerges with some sketches of clowns and some ideas about using glitter cloth from America on the top of the display drums and mirror cloth on the sides. The windows will be dressed out in magenta felt. For Christmas gift departments the idea of a fireplace with a clown seated beside it might add a seasonal touch.

After director-level approval comes the building of a mock-up in the studio. If then the theme looks destined to work, the job is put in hand. When the day comes for it to go in the window woe betide him if it is not ready and perfect! The display team rarely fails and its standard of presentation is one of the most obvious reasons visitors go home saying 'Have you seen Harrods? That's really something.'

It is easy for anything not constantly brought before the public eye to be forgotten. This applies to Harrods as to anything else and the press officer exists to ensure that there is plenty of publicity about Harrods in the papers and magazines and talk on radio and television. The more reference that is made in the press to merchandise available at Harrods the better. This is particularly true if the store has something special in the offing such as a promotion, a sale, a fashion show or a Christmas season.

The world of the press officer is often seen as glamorous and exciting but the reality is somewhat different; that is not to say the job is not exciting and interesting – it is, but it is also very hard work and much more effort goes into disciplined attention to detail than to heady rushes of inspiration. It is a world where normal working hours seem to go by the board and the press officer has to be on call pretty well night and day.

A typical day would start with a photography session in the food halls at 8.00 a.m. An American glossy magazine is doing a feature on Harrods. The store only allow this when there are no customers around as Harrods feels strongly about protecting the privacy of its customers. So the photographs have to be done then and as it is the press officer's job to accompany anyone taking photographs in the store she must be there.

She might get back to her office at 9.05. One of her three assistants is busily searching through a pile of all the daily papers for any mentions of Harrods, which are cut out and pasted into a press clippings book, in which can be found every article that has mentioned Harrods in the last few years.

The second is wrestling with a mound of assorted merchandise to be sent out to various journalists and editors in the hope that they will then do a write up in their publications.

The third has the telephone receiver wedged between her left ear and shoulder and is heaping sugar into four steaming mugs of coffee at the same time. The call will be from someone like the William Hickey column wanting to know if it is true that Lord So and So's daughter is really working in the Toy Fair for Christmas. The answer is usually 'yes'.

The press officer decides to go and see what is new in the

pet shop. Her excuse is that it is an area that frequently provides good copy for the papers; the real reason is that she is dotty about puppies and kittens. However, today she gets her story; the pet shop is doing a brisk trade in dog umbrellas and dog tee shirts. 'I only bought them for a laugh,' says the amazed buyer, 'and they are going bananas about them.'

She hurries back to her office; she must get the press on to the dog story before the pet shop sells out. As she enters the office number two greets her:

'Thank goodness you're back, *Cosmopolitan* wants to know if the story about the salesgirl in the fur department is true. What's the story anyway?'

'Oh, a new girl in the fur department forgot to write a bill for a £6,000 coat and so they billed all their regular customers in the hope that they would find the right one.'

'Did they?' asks number two.

'No, the whole lot paid up without a murmur.'

'Is it true then?'

'No, of course not, and what's more if you ever let anybody so much as hint that it's true the MD will have me on toast for breakfast; tell them categorically once and for all that it's a complete fabrication.'

Meanwhile number three is trying to answer a letter from a little girl in Ireland who has written in to Father Christmas asking him if he can feed her pony on his way through on Christmas Eve as she will be over at her Granny's on that night!

Another telephone clamours. It is the hat shop buyer wanting to know if it is all right to talk to the *Daily Mail* who wish to do an article about the comeback of hats on the fashion scene.

'Yes, fine, so long as I am there when you speak to them.'

No sooner does she ring off than another call comes through. The director of merchandise wants to talk about a forthcoming promotion and see how the press officer can get some editorial coverage for the merchandise which will be specially bought. Favourable editorial comment is strongly beneficial to the store and brings in customers. It is also free, unlike advertising.

And so it goes. Telephone calls to fashion editors, home editors, diary columnists, business page correspondents, news editors, overseas publications and radio and television companies and telephone calls from all the same people plus a host of enquirers wanting to know all manner of things about the store and many just using the Harrods Press Office as a general information centre, fill the day. Recently the telephone rang and it was a young man asking: 'What have you got on General Eisenhower?' Another call was from a lady enquiring urgently: 'I'm anxious to trace a narcissus with a name beginning with O and a rather sweet smell.' Much searching of catalogues in the florist department failed to produce the right name. True to Harrods tradition of service the assistant in the florist department offered an alternative. 'Oh, no,' replied the lady, 'I need the correct name for my crossword puzzle.'

At the south-western corner of the store opposite Walton Street is the entrance to the Hans Road receiving bank. The arch that affords access to the area is massive, for it was here that the first Richard Burbidge intended to build a 200-foot tower to celebrate the coronation of King George V in 1911. It was never built and today only a water tank sits astride the arch.

On weekdays the road outside the bank is usually cluttered with vehicles waiting to get in and unload their goods. Harrods has two other major receiving banks; one at Trevor Square and one at Barnes. Nevertheless the inflow of merchandise is so great that queues build up and the area daily takes on the semblance of a traffic warden's nightmare.

Once the merchandise is in the store, its first stop is in the marking off room, situated at the far end of the Brompton Road tunnel. The lower end of the two storeys deals with hardware goods and the upper storey is devoted to fashion in the main. The job done here is to check the merchandise and then to mark the price on the individual articles. Finally they clear the merchandise to the departments.

There are some departments that do not use the marking off room, for example the food halls and the pharmacy where the sheer volume dictates differently, but they do deal with around 160 of the 220 selling departments' merchandise. The nearby merchandise clearing room has a fleet of vehicles trundling round the store delivering new goods to all corners of the building.

Nearby is the returns room which is, as its name suggests, to where items are returned by the drivers if they are not able to deliver them for any reason.

Above the despatch 'ring' is the country despatch area, dealing with all deliveries outside the van delivery area. This may entail sending merchandise by post or by rail or carrier or even abroad by sea or air.

Back on ground level at Trevor Square on the north side of Brompton Road is a young man not likely to forget the name of Trevor Square. He applied for a job in the despatch department in the late 1960s and was directed to Trevor Square from the personnel department by the recruitment officer dealing with his application who finished by saying:

'—and when you get there, ask for Mr Nascimento.'

Mr Nascimento, the department manager, waited for the hopeful applicant to arrive. Minutes passed and gradually half an hour went past and still he did not appear. It was assumed he had thought better of his application and decided to go home. Not so, at 4.30 p.m., six and a half hours after the telephone call, a very exhausted young man appeared asking for Mr Nascimento. When it was established that he was in fact the young man sent by personnel in the morning Mr Nascimento enquired what had happened.

'Well, sir,' he replied, 'the lady in personnel told me to go to Trafalgar Square and ask for Mr Nascimento ...'

At Trevor Square is the traffic office, from where are

controlled the twenty-seven small parcel vans that do the town and suburban deliveries. Even though they do not go outside a thirty-five mile radius of central London they clock up $\frac{3}{4}$ million miles between them in a year.

The building at Trevor Square has five storeys and on the first floor is the silver factory, where craftsmen clean and engrave silver and undertake repairs. Also there is the trunks factory where Harrods still makes its own luggage and repair work is done. There are the tailoring workrooms. A little further along is the shoe repair factory where around 8,000 shoes are mended each year. Next door is the stationery warehouse. Until recently Harrods had its own stationery factory and prepared headed notepaper for customers. The service is still available but the work is contracted out. At the time that decision was made the store held about four hundred dies with the addresses of customers on which had to be sent to their owners. The dies are small metal blocks and the store started posting them in dozens. Twenty-four hours later the operation had to be halted as the dies were setting off GPO alarm signals at a time when letters bombs were prevalent.

The confectionery department stockroom is on the second floor. This area used to be the factory where Harrods chocolates were made but these now come from an exclusive outside manufacturer. Also on this floor is where the Christmas hampers are packed. The third floor is devoted to the Pantry warehouse and the fourth floor has the display studio along with the stockrooms for the toy department and Olympic Way. Finally, on the fifth floor, is the piano factory, the radio and TV warehouse and a rest room for the staff who work over at Trevor Square. On the roof is the carpenter's shop and the fibre glass workroom of the display department.

Part of the same division but geographically far removed are the furniture depositories down at Barnes. The building stands on the bank of the River Thames just east of Hammersmith Bridge. The commentary on the Oxford v Cambridge boat race often refers to the crews going past

Harrods. This can lead to mental images of the eights rowing down the Brompton Road if one is not aware of the Barnes depositories. Barnes is very much part of the store and is connected by a direct telephone link. Several of the 'big ticket' departments like furniture, carpets and major household appliances have bulk warehouses at Barnes so that, when the customer places an order the goods are sent out direct from Barnes. It is a considerable operation, handling several million pounds worth of merchandise each year.

The site also houses the auction galleries which are part of Harrods estate offices. A half-mile down Londsdale Road is Mill Lodge which is the premises of the Harrodian Club. An old country mansion set in fourteen acres of grounds, it was bought by the first Richard Burbidge as a sports and recreation club for the staff. Membership costs House of Fraser employees the princely sum of 10p per week; ammenities include tennis, squash, swimming, rugby, soccer, cricket, snooker, table tennis and darts and there is a thriving amateur dramatics society. The club is also the starting and finishing point for an annual sponsored walk undertaken by London's stores in aid of the 'Cottage Homes' which is an organization which houses retired people from the retail trade who are in need. With many of the trade's suppliers providing generous sponsorship the event raises well in excess of £25,000 each year.

The division of the store which includes Trevor Square and Barnes is indeed the division of the backroom boys but the contribution they make to the smooth running of the business cannot be overrated and many of the letters of praise that the store receives concern the rapid delivery of merchandise wanted for specific occasions.

CHAPTER SIX

Harrods Limited

Who owns Harrods? Frequently it is erroneously presumed that it is owned largely by middle eastern interests and from time to time rumours abound that someone is moving in on Harrods. During the 1970s there was talk of a merger with the Boots group, a strong American interest came and went, and 1980 started with further rumblings in the financial press.

The House of Fraser itself became the subject of take-over speculation when Lonrho acquired a substantial holding in the business in the late 1970s. As this book went to press a takeover bid had just been made by Lonrho during a dramatic board meeting held at the London headquarters of the House of Fraser. Hugh Fraser, later Lord Fraser of Allander, gained control of the Harrods group in a famous take-over battle in 1959, a story that is well detailed elsewhere, and since that time Harrods has belonged fair and square to the House of Fraser.

The House of Fraser is, by a considerable margin, the largest department store group in the country. It consists of seven major subsidiary groups of stores: House of Fraser (Northern) in Scotland, with stores such as Fraser's itself in Glasgow and other notable stores such as Arnotts and Daleys; the Binns Group in the North East; the House of Fraser (Midlands) trading as Rackhams in Birmingham and surrounding areas and as Kendal Milne in Manchester and Cavendish House in Cheltenham; the Dingles Group in the West Country and trading as Howells in Cardiff; the Army and Navy Group in London and the South East and including Barkers of Kensington which was the first store Hugh Fraser acquired in London; the Chiesmans

Group in the South East and East Anglia; and finally the Harrods Group trading in the London area under its own name at Knightsbridge, as D. H. Evans in Oxford Street and Wood Green and as Dickins and Jones in Regent Street, Richmond and shortly at Milton Keynes.

The groups are coordinated by a management committee which meets every month under the chairmanship of the managing director of the House of Fraser. The management structure of the store itself is inevitably complex but is perhaps best illustrated starting with the person the customer meets, that is the sales assistant, and working upwards.

Sales assistants are supervised by the first rank of junior management, selling controllers, whose job it is to try and ensure customers receive the standard of attention and service that Harrods aims to provide, and also to take care of the administrative details such as ensuring the whole department does not go off to lunch at the same time and that holidays are staggered.

The next rung up the ladder is the assistant buyer but where the job of a controller ends and that of an assistant buyer begins is often a grey area, particularly as many of the smaller departments do not have both. Then there is the buyer who is regularly out of the department on buying trips and holidays and the assistant buyer is responsible for the smooth running of the department at those times.

The buyer is responsible for the performance of his or her department, from the purchase of the merchandise to its sale to stock levels, pricing margins and gross profit, and for the staff. In some of the larger departments the job becomes too big for one and the responsibility for buying the merchandise and selling it is divided. The person put in charge of the selling end of the operation is called the department sales manager.

Departments are grouped into sections and the next level up is section manager. Taking the Man's Shop as an example there is a buyer for suits, one for shirts and ties, one for shoes and some others but the section manager of the Man's Shop has responsibility for the whole area.

The section manager reports to the divisional manager who has responsibility for the division of which there are six:

the food halls, the rest of the ground floor excluding the Central Hall, ladies fashion, the children's shop, Way In and the Central Hall, home furnishings including the second and third floors and Olympic Way and Way In Living, and a division consisting of the restaurants and the rest of the fourth floor not already specified.

There are five non-selling divisions, structured in a similar manner, which are: customer services, personnel and training, the counting house, i.e. the money side of things, store services and advertising and press relations. Two other important functions are security and display and they report straight to a director.

CHAPTER SEVEN

The sale of the century

"Tickets for the sale, guv ... only £100 each to you."

5.00 a.m. The dew sparkles in the dawn sunlight and the mist drifts lazily in and out of the hedgerows of East Anglia. The man crouching uncomfortably overlooking the road which winds below is chilled. He has been there for over an hour watching daylight creeping across the land.

He sees the vehicle as soon as it rounds the bend in the road below. Soon the little van will be in range and this time he will make no mistake. His eyes narrow as he finds the van through the telescopic sights and he runs his tongue round his lips in an involuntary expression of the tension gripping his body. The Harrods logo stands out clearly on the side of the vehicle as it whirrs along the road propelled at a leisurely pace by its electric motor; it is a Walker van, the only one of its type in the world. The man lying in wait high above zooms in on his victim; his knuckles whiten, he squeezes and the camera begins to roll.

The driver of the van is cursing through chattering teeth; it is the fourth time he has driven along the stretch of road this morning. Something has gone wrong on each of the other three occasions and he is so cold and exasperated that he is on the point of giving up altogether.

The take is almost over, it has gone perfectly. The light has been just right and the camera director knows he has obtained as perfect a picture as he is ever likely to get. The van rounds the last curve and trundles along the final hundred yards. 'Home and dry,' thinks the man at the controls; he is the chief engineer at Harrods and he is driving the van himself for it is his pride and joy and he will let no one else touch it. A smile spreads across his face and his teeth stop chattering to permit a heartfelt sigh of relief to escape. After a week of incidents they have got what they came for; a fifteen second television commercial for the Harrods sale.

That ratio between time and effort on the one hand and end result on the other seems to be about par for the course where Harrods is concerned; the sale lasts at fever pitch for only one or two days and goes on only for two or three weeks but it takes months of thought and preparation to launch it. It now is very big business indeed and the whole operation is mounted with military precision. Robert Midgley, the man who has given the word 'sale' an entirely new meaning in Harrods, has often been known to liken the twice yearly exercise to planning and fighting a battle.

The cash register stations must be secured against the incoming tide of customers. Experienced employees are put into the front line on the day whilst an army of temporary employees thrown in at the last moment are used carefully so that they don't break up under the extreme pressure of the first day. The rewards are sweet indeed; takings on the first day alone are counted in millions of pounds and each year sees that figure increase.

It is difficult to pinpoint the exact moment when the store begins to think about a sale; probably it is during the dying moments of the preceding one as buyers survey their shattered departments and note that they still have things left which they had hoped to get rid of and which they will now have to live with until they can put them into the next sale. Or the next ... They can change the display time after time to try and sell the offending merchandise and still it sits there. One option is to put a 'spiv' on it; that is a financial reward to the person who sells it. Another option is to keep reducing the price but the ultimate humiliation is to put it on the stand nearest the door and leave it unattended and nobody will steal it.

The next time any serious attention is given to a sale is when the managing director holds a meeting of his management team some two or three weeks after the end of the preceding sale to analyse the results; each year something new is learned and some further fine tuning takes place.

The same managers meet again six to eight weeks before the start of the next sale when the director of merchandise confirms the trading targets and there is usually a ripple of comment as the full extent of the campaign ahead is realized. The divisional managers of the selling departments give a run-down of the merchandise they will be offering and the state of readiness of their staff.

Perhaps on the ground floor there will be some particularly good value suits, a strong line in toiletries and the customary range of special offers throughout the fashion accessories and perfumery areas. The fashion floor may offer a once in a lifetime bonanza of dresses; they may decide to repeat the successful innovation of a blue sash for staff as sometimes it is difficult to tell the difference between the staff and the customers. Old hands will tell you that it is really quite easy when you get to learn the secret; the staff are the well dressed ones.

The home furnishings division often provides a seemingly bottomless pit of towels, sheets, blankets, table cloths and a particularly attractive offer on duvets; carpets might chip in with generous discounts on quality Wilton; and of course the china and glass sales in the fashion theatre on the third floor are usually enormous. There could be a particularly good offer on colour televisions, and so on.

The chief accountant confirms details of the arrangements for cash handling – the provision of extra tills around the store and adjustments to sanction limits on accounts. The major credit card companies send in people to set up on-line terminal link-ups with their head office computers to enable transactions to be approved with the minimum of delay. Details are given about the extra staff to be recruited, 1,000 of them, and they will all have to be trained and deployed in just a few days. Details, such as the fact that there will be an army of cleaners in the store the Sunday after the first sale Saturday to clear up the debris and repair the ravages of the day before, are fixed.

One of the most vital parts of any sale is the advertising, with coverage in the UK, on the Continent and even in the Middle East. The window displays have to be as professional as ever and the sale tickets ready in time. Security arrangements need to be comprehensive and the normal procedure will be adopted to ensure all doors open simultaneously. The course is now set and there can be no retreat. Always there are crises beyond the control of the store to be dealt with in this period. Perhaps a dock strike in Italy delays merchandise or the Chancellor may change the rate of VAT and throw calculations into chaos.

The Harrods sale is always a genuine sale, that is to say that the merchandise on offer is either the store's normal stock reduced in price or it is stock bought in especially for the sale and clearly marked as such. The aim is that the customer has the opportunity to buy good merchandise at a

more competitive price than can normally be offered as
well as that excess stock can be cleared.

As the day approaches the jigsaw is pieced together and
merchandise floods in. Clothes ... accessories ... china ...
glass ... furniture ... pots and pans ... records ... cookers,
televisions, carpets, sports equipment, fabrics, wines ...
every conceivable type of merchandise from a pin to an
elephant ... well almost! Meanwhile, the money men plan
how to have the millions of pounds taken in one form or
another on the first day counted, checked, bagged, collected
from the departments and despatched to the clearing banks.
Five hundred registers have to be positioned and an
operator and reliefs allocated to each one. Every year the
money men think that saturation point has been reached
and that it is just not possible to take or move any more
money.

In January the training department is faced with starting
one thousand people in three days; or 333 per day with the
maximum number that the training department will hold
being 220. That means that 113 people have to be kept in
transit at any one time which is an operation that requires
split second timing, a strong nerve and extremely thick
skins.

On the night before the first day of the sale, the managing director does a final tour of inspection to make sure all
is ready, talks to the buyers, looks at their displays of
merchandise and gives them some final words of encouragement. Gradually the clamour and the bustle die down, the
store falls silent, the security men roll down the fire doors.

The morning dawns! Queues have formed at all the
doors but Harrods vans parked nose to tail outside each
door help to contain the situation. It is not unknown for
some of the more enthusiastic bargain hunters to try slipping in through the staff entrance but they never make
first base as security is good. The hour from 8.00 to 9.00
wears on, the 6,000 staff arrive and gradually the cash
registers are switched on; one year recently they were *all*

switched on at 9.00 a.m., and the Harrods generators couldn't cope! The chief engineer still bears the scars from that occasion.

The minutes tick by and the queues begin to agitate and jostle. Inside the store the public address system blares out military music but nobody knows who is responsible for this as the culprit refuses to own up in the interest of his own safety. The security men take up their positions, the general manager looks at his watch and checks his transmitter. All the doors must open simultaneously and he will count down over his transmitter so that the security men at each entrance will know the moment.

Ten ... nine ... eight ... seven ... the security men join in ... six ... five ... four ... the crowd at door number five joins in ... three ... two ... one ... SCRAMBLE, for furs, china, glass, dresses, shirts, shoes, furniture, freezers,

"Good Lord, Wilkins, is it nine o'clock already?"

hi-fi, and anything and everything else under the sun. The management can only stand and watch and wait for the tornado to blow itself out.

Over the years many Harrods 'stories' have emerged. Nobody knows which are true and which are the products of fertile imaginations but one concerning the sale is particularly nice.

Evidence of good research done in advance involved a 'gentleman' in the kitchenware sale in the early 1970s. At that time the cashiers who worked the tills on the first day of the sale used to be allocated from the central cashier's office so that members of a given department rarely knew the cashier on their till. Furthermore extra cash registers are installed in busy sale departments to ease congestion. And of course many staff are sale temporaries. It was such a set of circumstances. He acquired a cash register similar to those used at that time, an identical trolley for moving cash registers around the store and finally a Harrods staff badge. He then wheeled the cash register into the store thence to the department and unloaded it on to the table at the end of the line of existing cash registers; he plugged it into the electricity supply and started taking money. In due course the register would hold no more and he turned to two nearby assistants and asked them to help him move the register back on to the trolley; they obliged and he trundled his booty out of the department. It is known what happened since the unfortunate gentleman was caught by the security staff leaving the store.

And so the morning wears on. The crowds rampage through the selling floors; husbands lose their wives, mothers lose their children and the escalator landings clog up with people.

There are plenty of arguments between customers but by and large tempers are remarkably controlled considering the claustrophobic circumstances. Neatly folded rows of merchandise disintegrate into great heaps of chaos as bargain hunters rummage and discard; the fitting rooms are sweaty with swarms of bodies ripping clothes on and off. Queues form for the restaurants as hunger and fatigue set in. A table collapses in the Man's Shop under the sheer weight of numbers pressing against it. Tills jam, account stamping machines become buried under mounds of merchandise and one or two deserters from the ranks of both the customers and the staff are observed furtively sloping off to the comparative calm of surrounding Knightsbridge. Camouflaged as normal human beings they can lie low out there for a while to allow time for their ears to recover from the clatter of crashing china.

Lunchtime approaches and brings the first indications of whether the sale is going well. Camera crews from the BBC and ITV and seemingly almost every European television company record the progress of the battle and all usually agree that traffic is even heavier than it was last sale. The afternoon brings no let-up. The temperature soars and the engineers work desperately to try to keep the store cool. The roof and basement are crawling with blue-overalled men running up and down iron ladders turning valves on and off to seemingly little avail.

The telephone switchboard is jammed with calls; the ladies' toilet runs out of water; fuses and lights blow and one of these years the sprinklers are going to turn themselves on. The security office has plenty of shoplifters and pick-pockets to deal with and there is a steady stream making the depressingly well worn pilgrimage to Chelsea Police Station via the store's investigators office in the basement.

As the afternoon wears on the clamour of the morning subsides a little. The managers and staff go to tea in relays and sit exhausted asking each other how it has gone, needing reassurance, wanting to tell someone what happened to them. And so they get the energy to face the last leg, up until 6.00 p.m.

The management decided in 1974 that a security man should be placed at the entrance to each gentlemen's toilet for the whole of the first day of the ensuing January sale since the bomb which did explode in the store (p. 55–6) was

assembled in the men's toilet. The first day wore on and
the uniformed officer on duty at the second floor men's
room, which is between the linens and books departments,
decided that he would stand just inside the outer double
swing doors. For those unfamiliar with the architectural
delights of this loo there are two sets of swing doors through
which one has to pass and a small square space in between.
This seemed an admirable spot from which to keep an eye
on things and by 5.00 p.m. the uniformed officer was standing staring with glazed eyes into the middle distance when
the outer doors opened and an exhausted looking lady
entered. Some funny things happen on the first day of the
sale and the officer decided to await further developments
before plunging in at the embarrassing deep end. She
put her numerous purchases down with a heartfelt sigh
and looked expectantly at the nonplussed officer. Fifteen
seconds passed and the lady grew impatient. Her accent and
tone when she spoke was pure Penelope Keith. Raising her
eyebrows and her chin, her voice scythed through the moth-
ball scented air: 'Well,' she hissed, 'are we going up or
down?'

And so to closing time. The final cash collection is done,
the staff who just came for the day are paid, and the buyers
and department managers survey the wreckage and decide
to put it out of their mind until Sunday when many of
them will be in to clean up. Amongst other things they have
to count the takings to arrive at what is called the flash
figure for the day, which is handed into the divisional
office before they go home.

The sea of people in the store begins to head for the
exits. Both sets of escalators are turned to down and for
half an hour the world pours out of Harrods bringing the
Knightsbridge traffic to a juddering halt. At 6.00 p.m. most
departments will have one difficult customer, fractious
about the store closing early, and when finally herded out,
complaining loud and long about the falling standard of
service these days.

But at last all the customers are out and most of the

staff have gone too; only a hard core remains to cash up and put the dust covers on. The store seems eerily quiet, the most frequently heard sounds being the jangling of keys and 'Goodnight – see you on Monday.' By which time it is half past six and time for the senior managers to make their way to the managing director's office where they are met by his secretary who offers them smoked salmon sandwiches and, more importantly, a drink. The first managers there have non-selling functions. The conversation is spasmodic, punctuated by frequent outbursts of nervous laughter; nobody ventures a guess at the day's takings.

The tension rises as managers from the selling divisions arrive, some reporting good trading and others with disappointment written across their faces; which is the true picture? Estimates of a bonanza are hastily revised; spirits drop a notch or two and the impossible nature of the target is commented upon. Once all the managers have arrived and reported and the sums are done, the managing director steps forward. First come the congratulations and then the thanks for unstinting dedication given in preparation and in battle; and then come the figures. Harrods has taken over £5,000,000 in one day. It is a staggering sum.

One further ritual is dealt with. Each year the management runs a sweepstake on the figure; the money is put into one envelope and at this point the managing director announces the winner and presents the modest cash prize 'It's tax free you know,' he reminds the winner with a relish that only a true merchant can feel at such moments.

The party breaks up quickly. All are tired both physically and mentally. A few will go over to a local establishment of fine repute for a celebratory drink but most go straight home and sit in their armchairs and fall fast asleep. In the chief cashier's office the lights burn on; they are counting ... counting ... counting to £5,000,000.

CHAPTER EIGHT

Vital statistics
and useless information

This section of the book is a random compilation of facts and figures about the store; some of them concern matters which are vital to its survival while others are purely frivolous. No attempt has been made to put them into context. Whilst every effort has been made to ensure the accuracy of the information it is inevitable that in some cases a certain amount of informed guesstimating has taken place.

The building: the ground plan of Harrods covers $4\frac{1}{2}$ acres and there are five floors affording 14 acres of selling space and $8\frac{1}{2}$ acres of stockrooms, offices and back-up services. There are 75 to 80 display windows depending on how you count them (!) and the exterior is lit by 11,000 bulbs.

Equipment: There are 50 lifts in the store and 11 at Barnes; they cover 49,800 miles per year. There are 12 escalators excluding the new bank near Door 10 and they cover 42,536 miles each year at a running speed of 100 feet per minute. There are 500 clocks, 25,000 sprinkler heads, 197 hydrants, 841 extinguishers, 990 fire resisting doors and shutters, 2,226 heat sensors and 114 hose reels.

Power and water: Harrods draws its water from its own three wells, the deepest of which is 489 feet; 1979 water consumption was approximately 27,161,000 gallons and oil consumption 3,700,858 litres. The engine room produces 800 tons of steam per week and the weekly divisional managers' meeting much more. Electricity consumption in 1979 was 18,315,455 units of which approximately 70% was generated by the store's engine rooms. The air in the store is changed 8 times per hour and on a hot summer day $\frac{3}{4}$ million cubic feet or 31 tons of air is supplied to the store each minute.

Telephones: There are 140 incoming lines and 1,800 internal extensions and the switchboard receives approximately 10,000 calls every day rising to 16,000 at Christmas. There are 41 coin box telephones in the store.

Transport: The van fleet numbers approximately 80 vehicles. The 27 delivery vans belonging to town despatch cover an average of 26,000 miles per year without going outside a 35–mile radius of Central London. The two remaining electric vans have their batteries recharged overnight and can then go about 60 miles without a further charge; the greatest mileage recorded on one charge is 87 miles. There are a further 2,000 vehicles used inside the store for the internal transport of merchandise.

Stationery: In 1963 the store used 8,000 miles of string. By 1980 it was using only 2,500 miles of string but 1,500 miles of sellotape; the string and sellotape went round 250,000 boxes containing 355 miles of corrugated paper. 5,000,000 Harrods bags are used in a year and 5,000,000 carriers. The number of photocopies taken annually is 3,000,000.

Staff: The number of staff employed ranges from 4,000 to 6,000 depending on the time of year. Approximately 10,000 written applications for jobs are received each year and 12,000 interviews conducted. From these 5,000 people are employed, 700 don't turn up so 4,300 start. 20,000 references are taken up each year. In 1980 the youngest member of staff was born in 1964 and the oldest in the nineteenth century. Thereby hangs a tale. The computer does not recognize any but the twentieth century for the purposes of calculating dates of birth; hence it assumes that anyone born in 1898 was born in 1998 and includes them in lists of employees who are under 18 years of age. An amendment to the programme has now stopped this rather charming anachronism.

Sales

year	£
1850	1,000
1868	50,000
1889	500,000
1902	1,000,000
1957	15,000,000
1969	26,477,000
1979	145,000,000

The largest amount ever taken in one day up to 31 December 1981 was £5,018,120 on 10 January 1981.

The largest single cash sale ever made up to 31 December 1981 was one of £82,000.

That Harrods unlike other shops puts prices UP when it wants to move something is quite untrue. Contrary to the popular myth, Harrods' experience is that there are very few people with more money than sense in the Knightsbridge area although there are some hungry people around at Christmas time.

Sales of food in the last two weeks before Christmas, 1979, were:

55 tons Christmas puddings
50 tons of fresh beef
36 tons of whole hams
17 tons fresh English turkeys
11 tons whole and baby Stiltons

10 tons mincemeat
9 tons Harrods chocolates
3 tons Christmas cakes
7 tons Pick 'n' mix sweets
3 tons glacé fruits
$2\frac{1}{2}$ tons nuts
3 tons smoked salmon
$\frac{1}{4}$ ton caviar
65,000 mince pies
24,000 bottles Perrier water
and
96,200 headache pills

Harrods tomorrow

Fascinating as it is to look back at Harrods, it is business for tomorrow that is the major concern for the company that hopes to survive and prosper and grow. Department stores are facing tough times, together with the rest of the retail world, as the 1980s begin and inflation makes it difficult to provide the special services upon which department stores rely to attract custom whilst customers inevitably become value conscious.

It is sad to note that Harrods needs to spend ever increasing amounts to cut down losses due to theft. Every year the energy devoted to security of cash and merchandise increases which raises the prices for the honest customers, the ones that foot the bill in the form of higher prices.

Hard trading times mean that Harrods has to promote itself harder. At the economy end of the retail market this may well be done on price which can only be good for the consumer and already we have seen this starting in the motor trade as recession bites. In the case of Harrods more work will be put into hopefully improved promotions drawing attention to particular lines of merchandise. The store has always regarded itself as being in the entertainments business as well as the retail one and the trend will be directed increasingly at professionalism and display.

The store is confident that travel will continue to increase and it is now not enough for merchandise just to have come from abroad for it to be desirable. It will have to be special in its own right and the store's buyers face a stimulating task. The technology of electronics will not pass by the retail world. Point of sale equipment and stock control machines become more sophisticated and give the store a quicker idea of market trends. But Harrods cares greatly about its reputation for personal service and there is no danger of people becoming obsolete in the business.

The selling area of the store will continue to expand. The new bank of escalators at the west end of the building should open up that side to greater customer flow and it is inevitable that the west end of the fourth floor will be developed as a direct consequence. Then there is the whole of the fifth floor and don't forget the roof!

There is no doubt that amenities for the customers will have to get better. If people are to continue to go to the centre of town and spend the day shopping it must be made as attractive and enjoyable as possible for them. Harrods does not fear the competition of out of town shopping centres, believing that there is room for both as long as it does its job properly. Harrods will stick to its policy. There will always be room in the world for a department store offering true quality and value and to guard its reputation as the finest department store in the world Harrods must believe in itself and its legend.

Selected Bestsellers

☐	**The Amityville Horror**	Jay Anson	80p
☐	**The Health Food Guide**	Michael Balfour and	
		Ruby Rae	£1.50p
☐	**The Island**	Peter Benchley	£1.25p
☐	**Smart-Aleck Kill**	Raymond Chandler	95p
☐	**The Entity**	Frank De Felitta	£1.25p
☐	**Whip Hand**	Dick Francis	£1.50p
☐	**Solo**	Jack Higgins	£1.50p
☐	**The Rich are Different**	Susan Howatch	£1.95p
☐	**Moviola**	Garson Kanin	£1.50p
☐	**The Empty Copper Sea**	John D. MacDonald	90p
☐	**Where There's Smoke**	Ed McBain	80p
☐	**Spike Island**	James McClure	£1.95p
☐	**The Master Mariner**		
	Book 1: Running Proud	Nicholas Monsarrat	£1.50p
☐	**Bad Blood**	Richard Neville and	
		Julie Clarke	£1.50p
☐	**The Queen and Lord M**	Jean Plaidy	£1.50p
☐	**Fools Die**	Mario Puzo	£1.50p
☐	**Sunflower**	Marilyn Sharp	95p
☐	**The Throwback**	Tom Sharpe	95p
☐	**Wild Justice**	Wilbur Smith	£1.50p
☐	**That Old Gang of Mine**	Leslie Thomas	£1.25p
☐	**Caldo Largo**	Earl Thompson	£1.50p
☐	**Harvest of the Sun**	E. V. Thompson	£1.25p
☐	**The Third Wave**	Alvin Toffler	£1.95p

All these books are available at your local bookshop or newsagent, or can be ordered direct from the publisher. Indicate the number of copies required and fill in the form below

▬▬▬

Name_____
(block letters please)
Address_____

_____

Send to Pan Books (CS Department), Cavaye Place, London SW10 9PG
Please enclose remittance to the value of the cover price plus:

25p for the first book plus 10p per copy for each additional book ordered to a maximum charge of £1.05 to cover postage and packing
Applicable only in the UK

While every effort is made to keep prices low, it is sometimes necessary to increase prices at short notice. Pan Books reserve the right to show on covers and charge new retail prices which may differ from those advertised in the text or elsewhere